'There are times when one needs a jewel on a particular theme, an inspiration or a saying. At such moments *A Canopy of Stars* is a useful resource ... very accessible and timely, reminding us of the importance of continuing to ponder the eternal truths.'
Champagnat

'Presented in a witty and attractive manner, combining Gleeson's thoughts with a wide selection of wisdom from others ... He has a gift for finding the apt or inspirational quotation and weaving it in ... The quotations are always thought-provoking.'
Catholic Life

'This is the book's strength: seemingly simple ideas that open the doors for long contemplation, reflection personal challenge and prayer ... useful for both personal and group reflection on God's goodness to his people.'
The Mix

'This book is a collection of many wise minds and stories that have been used by Christopher Gleeson in his many addresses and messages to his school audiences – students, teachers and parents. It's a book you can open at any page and find something that resonates with your own inner ponderings and truths. It has a gem on every page and is a definite resource if you enjoy pertinent stories and wisdom of the ages. For parents of teenagers and teenagers themselves, it offers guidance in the form of encouragement and inspiration.'
Cornerstone

'It's the sort of book many people are looking for – brief, punchy and with some light for the journey. Much needed!'
Michael Whelan sm, Aquinas Academy

*Whenever she starred,
as she often did,
the gleaming of God
was showing through.*

Peter Steele SJ, in his homily at
the Mass of thanksgiving for
the life of Deirdre Rofe IBVM
27 August 2002

A Canopy of Stars

SOME REFLECTIONS FOR THE JOURNEY

A new and expanded edition

Christopher Gleeson SJ

David Lovell Publishing
Melbourne Australia

Revised and expanded edition
published in 2017 by

David Lovell Publishing
PO Box 44, Kew East
Victoria 3102 Australia
tel/fax +61 3 9859 0000
publisher@davidlovellpublishing.com

© Copyright 2003, 2017 Christopher Gleeson SJ.
Copyright in any individual extract or quotation is that of the individual author.

This work is copyright. Apart from any fair dealing for the purposes of private study, research, criticism or review, as permitted under the Copyright Act, no part may be reproduced by any process without written permission. Inquiries should be addressed to the publisher.

Cover illustration: The Milky Way, as seen from the Black Rock Desert, Nevada. Photo by Steve Jurvetson.
Design by David Lovell Publishing
Typeset in 12/15 Garamond Pro
This edition printed through Ingram Spark

National Library of Australia Cataloguing-in-Publication data
Gleeson, Christopher, 1943- author.
A canopy of stars : some reflections for the journey / Christopher Gleeson SJ.
  New and expanded edition
  ISBN: 9781863551618 (paperback)
  Includes bibliographical references.
  Quotations, English. Aphorisms and apothegms. Wisdom – Quotations, maxims, etc.

Author's Note
The extracts, quotations, and prose and poetry in this collection have been gathered over many years and from numerous sources. Every effort has been made to trace the source of the material used. We would appreciate any further information about sources we have not been able to trace.

Contents

Thirteen years on　　　　　　　　　　　　　　　　　　ix

Part 1
Eight Stars

Introduction　　　　　　　　　　　　　　　　　　　　3

Star one
Living in the shelter of each other　　　　　　　　　　13

Star two
Living with our feet on the ground and our eyes on the stars　35

Star three
Living is 90 per cent attitude　　　　　　　　　　　　51

Star four
Living as people of soul　　　　　　　　　　　　　　71

Star five
Living with success and failure　　　　　　　　　　　93

Star six
Living in the present　　　　　　　　　　　　　　　107

Star seven
Living with the Maker of the Stars　　　　　　　　　125

Star eight
Living on the move　　　　　　　　　　　　　　　155

Part 2
Four Canopies

Introduction	171
Canopy one Ensuring the proper perspective and balance in my life	177
Canopy two With Jesus on the road	195
Canopy three Jesus the lover	205
Canopy four God the giver and the gift	215
A not so final word	221
References	224

*This book is dedicated to
all those friends and colleagues,
many of them Heads of Schools,
who have been 'stars' for
my journey along the way.*

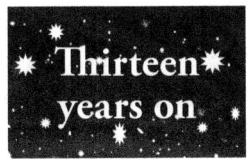

Thirteen years on

It is quite humbling to learn that this modest little tome is out of print and the publisher wants to re-publish it. To date some six thousand copies have found their way into homes, schools and parishes across the country, and it has been a delight to hear from people in various conferences and retreats that they prize it for ready reference. Indeed, let me quote from an email sent to me recently by someone who has had radical surgery for breast cancer:

> I've been meaning to write and thank you profoundly for the copy of your book, *A Canopy of Stars*. When I last returned [home] to Montana (mid-April), they decided I needed a heart implant, which happened at the end of April. During that surgery, they discovered a mass on my chest wall (a very grim area to find anything). That led to more surgery in June, where they found several masses. The wonderful news is that they were benign tumors, although having them at all is still a bit alarming. Anyhow, to make a long story longer (a core competency) …
> in the lead-up to the second surgery, when all the medicos were being disconcertingly somber, I found real solace at random moments during those 'waiting' days (the worst part) in picking up your book and reading sections/excerpts. I wasn't in a frame of mind to commit to some tome of (I'm sure) wordy, virtuous prose, but both the concise structure and lovely content of your book was literally heaven-sent and comforting for me. So, I cannot thank you sincerely enough for that beautiful gift in a bit of a dark time.

During the past thirteen years I have had four assignments from my Jesuit superiors. As Director of Jesuit Publications (now Jesuit Communications) for two years in Melbourne, I rejoiced in working with and learning from a team of splendid writers like Andrew Hamilton SJ. Never a word does Andy waste, and he writes so crisply and movingly across a huge range of topics.

In September 2005, I was assigned to Brisbane to begin what is now known as the Faber Centre of Ignatian Spirituality and in 2007, with the Provincial's permission, I applied for and obtained my first 'external' job as a Jesuit – Director of the new Santa Teresa Spirituality Centre in Ormiston, Brisbane. Indeed, I think there were more people on the interviewing panel than there were applicants for the position! When offered an extension of contract in 2010, I sought my new Provincial's permission to continue in that role, but he gently declined this request and asked me to return to Melbourne to be his Delegate for Education and later Mission Formation. His successor has now asked me to take on a new, full-time responsibility as his Delegate for Ignatian Formation.

The last ten years have seen me travelling almost every week – giving retreats and presentations to all sorts of Catholic and Christian groups. Indeed, Qantas and Virgin Airlines have constantly provided a seat for me to read copious books and articles of inspiration. In the year 2007, for example, my work took me to many parts of Queensland and, indeed, Australia – Albany Creek, Upper Coomera, Bundaberg, Gladstone, Rockhampton, Emerald, Longreach, Barcaldine, Mackay, Biloela, Gympie, Hervey Bay, Merrimac, Adelaide, Melbourne, Launceston, Perth, Cairns, Bateman's Bay, Toowong, Manly, Ormiston.

No wonder, then, that I could open my March 2014 editorial for *Madonna* with these words:

> In early December last year, when returning from Auckland, I stopped at the Tullamarine airport's duty-free shop to purchase

some spiritual sustenance for my Xavier Jesuit community. After discerning what spirit was most appropriate for my abstemious brethren, I went to the counter to pay for it. The young lady in attendance there greeted me with the question, 'Are you in transition, sir?' 'Yes', was my reply. 'Aren't we all?'

Thirteen years on, I am still an inveterate 'scavenger' of people's best thoughts and ideas – as Professor Greg Dening proclaimed in his book *Xavier Portraits* in 1992 – and I want to share a small selection of these newly-collected pearls by adding them to this book. They cover the period 2003-2016, and I present them under the four ample canopies of the four 'Weeks' or segments of the *Spiritual Exercises* of St Ignatius of Loyola. So in this book we now have eight Stars and four Canopies.

My hope is that something here might touch your heart as it has moved mine.

> I have a theory that only what touches the heart is really lodged in the mind. Memory is made up of what has touched our lives … We become those who have touched us.[1]

Christopher Gleeson SJ
December 2016

---

[1] Joan Chittister, *Called to Question: A Spiritual Memoir*, Sheed & Ward, 2004, pp. 152, 122.

Part 1

Eight Stars

Introduction

'However apart, we are together'

For all but eighteen months of the period 1981-2002, I was privileged to lead Jesuit school communities in both Melbourne and Sydney. As with all Heads of School, many words of reflection and recommendation have flowed from my pen and tongue during that time, and some of my listeners have generously encouraged me to assemble them in book form. This collection is a grateful response to that invitation and is dedicated to all those people who have been 'stars' for my journey along the way.

When writing about Xavier College in *Xavier Portraits* in 1992, Professor Greg Dening referred to me, rather unflatteringly I thought, as a 'scavenger' of others' ideas and sayings.[1] This book unashamedly confirms his view. Rather than use these treasures for my own private consumption, however, I have tried always to share with the wider educational community those written and spoken words which have touched my heart.

Indeed, the first of these reflections which I quote below comes from one of my Year 9 boarding students in 1999. When his parents showed me his letter home to them, I was much moved. While its grammar and spelling leave a little to be desired, it has served as something of the inspiration for the title of this book. Against the background of the recent death of a family friend ('Bucko', a much-loved old boy of the school and father of 'Charlie'), he wrote to his parents from his uninterrupted and well-publicized dormitory view of the heavens:

---

[1] Greg Dening and Doug Kennedy, *Xavier Portraits*, Old Xaverians Association, Melbourne, 1993, p. 338.

> Every night I gaze up and see three stars I have named the star [one] witch is called mum, star [two] witch is called dad, and star three witch I called [bucko] because of charlies sake and for bucko to help me through school in the hard times because he came here. But I am also looking for two more stars witch I will call poppy/courage and the other will be called pa/hope. I gave them these names because poppy was courageous because he went to war and I called pa/hope because he was farmer who had hope that rain would come in the future to help him. These are my five stars.

The other source of inspiration for this book derives from the following beautiful poem of Andrew Bullen sj which I quote in full here. He is writing about St Ignatius of Loyola, the founder of the Society of Jesus, who loved to look up in wonder at the star-studded Roman sky at night and contemplate the grandeur of the Creator and his creation. Like my young student author, Ignatius would name the stars after his Jesuit companions and friends spread out across the globe. What strong companionship and love there is in Andrew Bullen's beautiful words: 'However apart, we are together'!

Ignatius and the Stars

Lights there in the dark
flicker and go,
and come again.

Awake, alone in the sleeping house,
I have the stars for company.
What is light, I wonder?

God our Lord labours there:
the darkness (a vast, silent solace), those lights
flung out, are his exuberant work.

What is love? I wonder
and know. He is in the stars
and between them, and beyond.

Naming the stars is counting blessings,
is praise and thanksgiving.
Watching them move is slow

as prayer, as the rhythm
of the breathing of God our Lord.
Stars are seeds of light sown in darkness.

Watching them, I know
the dense clarity of light, of life, of love,
inside and outside.

There is light and light crucified
and light among us hovering.
Light speaks – to all of us, to me.

Contemplation gains love.
So make the heart an astrolabe
to reach the furthest star.

Xavier is Sirius, the brightest star,
he shines towards Cathay.
Bobadilla is the Bear:

this is the hearsay of the heavens.
Of the most distant stars I can say,
'They are companionable'.

My companions move in the universe;
the sky rings with their happiness;
their deeds are the interchange of light.

My companions are scattered
over all the world, where each can see the sky:
however apart, we are together.

> The voicing of their prayers,
> brimful of joy,
> echoes the music of the spheres.
>
> Far south, men claim, shines
> the Cross; let the configuration
> of the companions shine like that.
>
> Their shining makes a temple of me.
> The sun's rays fall on all my life:
> we are made holy places.
>
> The stars shine on Pamplona;
> on whichever of my pilgrim places they shine,
> they sign the way to Jerusalem.
>
> Even if I die alone,
> the stars will be my companions.
> Take, Lord, the heavens I have and possess …
>
> Take, Lord, and receive all my liberty,
> My memory, my intellect, and all my will
> – all that I have and possess.
> You gave it to me.
> To You, Lord, I return it.
> All is Yours, dispose of it
> according to Your will.
> Give me Your love and grace,
> for this is enough for me.[2]

In this book, I want to name some of the stars which have provided me with light and companionship for my journey over the past thirty plus years – in the hope that they can render the same service for others. Unlike the authors mentioned above, however, I will look on the stars

---

[2] Andrew Bullen, *Ignatius the Pilgrim: Poems for Prayer*, Jesuit Publications, Melbourne, 1992.

not as people, but as those nuggets of wisdom they have bequeathed to us for our journeying.

Why stars? I could have chosen another famous image – that of the lighthouse – which I have used many times to good effect in class and school assemblies. In elaborating what he terms 'lighthouse values and principles', Stephen Covey tells the following story in his excellent book, *The Seven Habits of Highly Effective People*:

> Two battleships assigned to the training squadron had been at sea on maneuvers in heavy weather for several days. I was serving on the lead battleship and was on watch on the bridge as night fell. The visibility was poor with patchy fog, so the captain remained on the bridge keeping an eye on all activities. Shortly after dark, the lookout on the wing of the bridge reported, 'Light, bearing on the starboard bow'. 'Is it steady or moving astern?' the captain called out. Lookout replied, 'Steady, captain', which meant we were on a dangerous collision course with that ship. The captain then called to the signalman, 'Signal that ship: We are on a collision course, advise you change course 20 degrees.' Back came a signal, 'Advisable for you to change course 20 degrees.' The captain said, 'Send, I'm a captain, change course 20 degrees.' 'I'm a seaman second class', came the reply. 'You had better change course 20 degrees.' By that time, the captain was furious. He spat out, 'Send, I'm a battleship. Change course 20 degrees.' Back came the flashing light, 'I'm a lighthouse.' We changed course.[3]

The meaning of this story is not lost on young people when it is explained that there are certain lighthouse values, lighthouse principles, in our lives which are immutable and rock solid in lighting our path. Covey also refers to them as 'true north' principles[4], because they have a

---

[3] Stephen Covey, *The Seven Habits of Highly Effective People: Restoring the Character Ethic*, Information Australia, Melbourne, 1990, p. 33.

reality independent of us – 'north' remains 'north' whatever our disposition or opinion. 'Principles … don't depend on the behaviour of others, the environment, or the current fad for their validity. Principles don't die. They aren't here one day and gone the next. They can't be destroyed by fire, earthquake or theft.'[5]

Professor Max Charlesworth once captured this beautifully in the following statement: 'Some things are *true* whether we think so or not; some things are *good* whether they suit our interests or not; some things are *just* whether or not they go counter to what we immediately want; some things are *beautiful* whether we happen to like them or not; some things are *sacred* whether we are willing to recognize them or not.'[6]

Stars, lighthouses, true north images. I could have used also Bruce Chatwin's beautiful picture of 'song lines', so much a part of the spirituality of Australia's Indigenous people. In his book of the same name he writes:

> Each totemic ancestor, while travelling through the country, was thought to have scattered a trail of words and musical notes along the line of his footprints, and … these Dreaming-tracks lay over the land as 'ways' of communication between the most far-flung tribes. 'A Song', Arkady said, 'was both map and direction-finder. Providing you knew the song, you could always find your way across the country.'
>
> 'And would a man on "Walkabout" always be travelling down one of the Songlines?'
>
> 'Yes!'

Isn't this a beautiful description of what we teachers and parents are trying to do in forming the young people in our care? By endeavour-

---

[4] Stephen Covey, *First Things First*, Simon & Schuster, New York, 1994, p. 51.
[5] ibid., p. 122.
[6] M. Charlesworth, 'Liberal education and religious values', an address at the University of Western Australia, 24 April 1988, p. 2.

ing to communicate lighthouse values and true north principles, are we not trying to scatter a trail of words and musical lines along the line of our footprints – songlines which, like lighthouses, are both maps and direction-finders?

I have opted, however, to use the image of stars in this book. There is an accessibility and companionability about them, an affinity with them even on the blackest of nights which I find alluring. Indeed, it is important to remember that the stars shine at their brightest in the darkest of night skies. Not only do they light up the darkness, but they are, in the words of that wonderful song from the musical *Les Misérables*, 'the sentinels silent and sure keeping watch in the night'. There is a constancy and immutability about the stars, 'filling the darkness with order and light', ever watching over us and illuminating our path through life.

While travelling in North Cornwall in early 2003, I went into a shop in the beautiful little fishing village of Padstow to look at some antiques. It was a bitterly cold day and I was rugged up with a beanie and scarf covering much of my face. When he caught sight of me, the shopkeeper quipped: 'Is anyone at home in there?' It is a good question, because often we are anywhere but at home to ourselves.

As a homecoming exercise, reflection is a powerful tool for all of us. It is that capacity to stop and ponder the meaning of our experiences and the direction of our life. It is the ability to place a mirror on our actions and reflect back to ourselves the value of our activities. Far too frequently, we allow life to wash over us. As the great Brazilian Archbishop Helder Camara said: 'Action alone without reflection is being busy pointlessly.' If it is accurate to describe our teaching ministry in schools as a ministry of meaning, we need to help ourselves and our young people to be reflective. 'We progress by stopping', wrote Meister Eckhart, the great German Dominican preacher of the thirteenth century.

T. S. Eliot once described contemporary human beings as being 'distracted from distraction by distraction' and we are certainly distracted today by superficial living. Our consumer life-style keeps mystery at bay and wants to keep us and our young people on the move, to live life on the surface. Why else could the seats at fast food places be so hard, if not to keep us on the move?

Back in 1949, the distinguished German theologian Paul Tillich wrote, 'Most of our life continues on the surface. We are enslaved by the routine of our daily lives, in work and pleasure, in business and recreation. We do not stop to look at the height above us, or the depth below us … We talk and talk and never listen to the voices speaking to our depth and from our depth. We accept ourselves as we appear to ourselves, and do not care what we really are. Like hit and run drivers, we injure our souls by the speed with which we move on the surface; we miss, therefore, our depth and true life.'[7] Very little has changed in the past sixty years.

Observant readers of this little volume of reflections will note that a disproportionate share of coverage is given to my time at St Ignatius' College, Riverview, from mid-1993 to November 2002. Although I spent a longer period as Head of Xavier College in Melbourne from 1981 to 1991, computers were a mystery to me until the staff presented me with one as a farewell gift. The preponderance of Riverview quotations from the weekly newsletter 'Viewpoint', therefore, acknowledges that my reflections during this latter period were both more recent and saved for perpetuity on computer files.

I want to record my thanks to those who gave me a home where I could compile these reflections – my brothers Tony and Tim, and their wives Mary and Maree; and my Jesuit family in Dublin with Bruce Bradley SJ and the wonderfully hospitable Jesuit community at Brophy

---

[7] Quoted in Hedley Beare, 'The Journey Inwards: The Journey Outwards', an address delivered at St Leonard's College Speech Night, 1982.

College Preparatory in Phoenix, Arizona. In thanking Carla James for compiling a CD of my 'Viewpoint' reflections, I want also to express my gratitude to those good people who found time to read the text and offer comments for its improvement – Bob Grant, Peter Quin sj, Trish O'Brien (who coined the title of the book), Philip Wallbridge, Annie McNamara, Margaret Scanlon, Bebe McEncroe and Michael Green. I hope also that I have satisfied their wish for including more of my own personal experience, so much of which as a student and staff member derives from the living spirit and traditions of the Society of Jesus founded by St Ignatius of Loyola in 1540.

Apart from this Introduction, each chapter in this first section of the book will focus on one star to light up our journey. It will carry with it an introductory reflection to develop and elucidate the theme, followed by a broad assortment of reflective comments by various authors, some known, some anonymous.

May the words of this book be a light for your path and enable you to be a star for all those who travel with you.

Stars

In places where air still offers clarity,
stars sing a siren song from space
in the bright night.

Lying on soft earth,
carried into sky by longing,
humans respond to stars
with questions. Why is the Universe
so vast? Why are we so small?

Call and response through the night.

My whole life I have sent
these questions into space. And
listened for response.

Then sky wakens and star song fades.
Humans forget mystery and get on with living.
But the stars, the stars
keep calling. No response.
Why is it that we call to
stars with science and insignificance?

On the next bright night,
find the clear air and ask again.
Humans, ask again. Who are we?
What is our place in mystery?

Perhaps you will hear what I
have heard, a song of inner
radiance.

For the stars
the stars are calling

saying we must
turn to one another
turn to one another and see
finally see
the stars everywhere.

Note: In a clear night sky, for every star we see, there are 50 million more behind it.[8]

---

[8] Margaret J. Wheatley, *Turning to One Another: Simple Conversations to Restore Hope to the Future*, Berrett Koehler, San Francisco.

Living in the shelter of each other

*'He decides the number of the stars
and gives each of them a name.'*
Psalm 147:4

'We live in the shelter of each other', the old Irish proverb says. What a splendid image! School principals and their staff are constantly challenging their students to look out for each other in the school community. Caring for one another is what strong communities do. Indeed, the quality of any community can be measured by the care it provides for its weakest members. 'None of us is as strong as all of us' was at one time the clever catch-cry of fast food giant McDonald's. What a difference it would make to our world if we could all adopt the African philosophy of happiness expressed in the adage, 'I am because we are'!

In schools we sometimes talk about the 'hidden curriculum', the 'informal curriculum', the 'implicit curriculum' – that is, everything a school teaches outside the formal classroom simply because of the kind of place it is. Punctuality, a willingness to work hard on tasks that are not immediately enjoyable, the importance of courtesy and respect for difference of every kind – these qualities are not part of the formal curriculum, but they are taught at school in so many ways every day.

During recent years, schools have worked extremely hard to eliminate from their communities bullying in all its various and sinister forms. It is one of those demons that needs to be exorcized because it is so alien to the building of community. Heads and other school administrators should not be afraid to name and claim bullying in their schools. Far from airing one's dirty linen in public, to name and claim it is to take the first steps towards disempowering it. In my experience, programs to eradicate bullying have been more successful where a positive value has been the projected target. In other words, rather than simply assemble an 'anti-bullying' project as such, focusing on something like developing 'respect for difference' has given these programs' activities clearer direction and hence greater energy. After all, community is the place where we learn to value and respect each other, even if we don't always get our own way or have our needs met. Here we learn that life is about us, and not just about me. Community is that place where we learn to value and honour people with whom we might not always get along. Community, above all, is the place where we respect and celebrate our differences.

Young people first learn about community in the shelter of their family. What they learn or fail to learn in the home they bring with them to the wider community of the school family. Not surprisingly, then, many of the reflections in this chapter point to the crucial importance of strong interaction and understanding between home and school.

Social researchers like Hugh Mackay have opened our eyes to the fact that at least 50 per cent of Australian households now contain only one or two people.[1] Despite the great importance which Australians attach to the traditional ideals of family life,[2] it is clear that the acceptance of de facto marriages, blended families, step-families, and single-parent families will bring further change in family structures in this country.

Not all of this change has been for the better. If it is accurate to talk generally about the erosion of the family and family values in Australia, then it is going to be extremely difficult for a young person to

---

[1] Hugh Mackay, *Re-Inventing Australia: The Mind and Mood of Australia in the 90s*, Angus & Robertson, Sydney, 1993, p. 77.
[2] A. Vanden Heuvel, 'The Most Important Person in the World', in *Family Matters*, August 1991, no. 29, pp. 8-13.

learn any values at all. Rabbi Jonathan Sacks, former Chief Rabbi of the Commonwealth, was absolutely right when he said that 'it is precisely as the member of a community that I learn a moral language, a vision, and its way of life. I become articulate by acquiring a set of meanings not of my own invention, but part of a common heritage.'[3] The family is the crucial unit in providing this common heritage within the wider community we know as society.

To achieve this community-building there is some value in using the metaphor of 'team' to describe how the family might best function. Research of teams in companies has shown that 'a team is a small number of people with complementary skills, who are committed to a common purpose, a common set of performance goals and approach, for which they hold themselves mutually accountable.'[4] If we put aside the managerial imagery for the moment, this definition does point to the fact that there must be a clear framework of expectations for a group of people to collaborate and cooperate effectively. Extensive research done on children's development has shown that two broad factors are essential for their proper socialization – 'a warm and accepting environment, and the exercise of consistent controls which limit the child's behaviour and gradually allow the exercise of independence within accepted social guidelines.'[5]

Family rules and regulations, therefore, should be expressed in terms of preserving the positive values which are respected and agreed to by all members of the family. They should be an expression of agreed family attitudes and standards of mutual respect and support. In this way the family operates closely as a team and provides the security and sense of being safe which children need.

---

[3] Jonathan Sacks, *The Persistence of Faith: Religion, Morality, and Society in a Secular Age*, The Reith Lectures 1990, Weidenfeld & Nicolson, London, 1991, p. 45.

[4] From an article entitled 'The Wisdom of Teams' in *Harvard Business Review*, March-April, 1993.

[5] Don Edgar, 'The School's Role in Promoting Family Life', *IARTV Occasional Paper*, June 1990, no. 15, p. 1.

There is no doubt that a healthy family life runs counter to the 'supermarket' morality prevalent in society today. In this tepid moral climate which canonizes the possession of options above all else, how often do we hear phrases like 'It's all right if I believe it to be', or 'It's my choice and if it's my choice it can't be wrong'! There has been a huge slide in our language when the word 'examine' comes to mean 'negotiate', a human 'right' equals a 'preference', 'love' means 'like', 'be good' is the same as 'feel good', and 'think logically' comes to mean 'feel comfortable with'.

Many people have come to measure morality simply by their own subjective feelings, because they have substituted taste and sentiment for hard thinking about what is right and wrong. It is not surprising, then, to hear opinions like 'To each his own.' 'Everybody is different, so morals are different for everybody.' 'It isn't up to me to tell anyone how to live.' 'If I think it's okay, it's okay for me, but maybe not for others.' To make moral judgments about what is right and wrong in this Frank Sinatra climate of 'I did it my way' is denigrated as judgmental. Calling a way of life wrong is an assault on the integrity or authenticity of others.[6]

Is it not time to return to those objective values of rights and obligations which impose themselves on us? Have we not forgotten, or neglected to point out in our classrooms that the right to express an opinion does not mean that the opinion is right. Is it not time to abandon the wishy-washy teaching which prefaces classroom discussions with words like 'There are no right or wrong answers here – I do not want to impose my values on you'?

I believe that a healthy family, which is striving to establish the sort of clearly agreed controls and expectations elaborated above, can be a wonderful avenue for counteracting all the evils of the so-called 'supermarket' morality. Jonathan Sacks puts this very succinctly when he says:

---

[6] Jonathan Sacks, op. cit., p. 42.

At every stage the concept of the family stands counter to the idea of unrestricted choice. To be a child is to accept the authority of parents one did not choose. To be a husband or wife is to accept the exclusion of other sexual relationships. To be a parent is to accept responsibility for a future that I may not live to see. Families only exist on the basis of choices renounced. And our secular culture has made that voluntary closure of options hard to accept or even understand.[7]

It is an important truism that there must be a synergy between families and schools to ensure, in the words of one school council member with whom I worked, that we are all singing from the same song sheet. There must be a resonance, nay consonance, of values between home and school if young people are to grow up hearing consistent and strong messages about right values. In this context I have always found challenging the words of Professor Greg Dening in his book *Xavier Portraits*, mentioned in the Introduction: 'A school confronts a never-to-be-resolved contradiction. It must fulfil the expectancies of those it serves, if it is to survive. It must change those expectancies, if it is to be truly educational.'[8] This advice reminds me of the provocative American bishop who was quoted in the press as stating that 'the church exists to comfort the afflicted and to afflict the comfortable.'

In April 1982, I published the following reflection by a British Jesuit educator, asking whether Jesuit schools would have the courage to utilize this rather bold statement as their school prospectus:

> We try to help our pupils to attach a very low priority to material possessions beyond basic necessities, and to achieve a total indifference to matters of status.
>
> We want them to be able to criticize the society in which they live objectively, temperately, and, if need be, ruthlessly.

---

[7] Jonathan Sacks, op. cit., p. 56.
[8] Greg Dening and Doug Kennedy, *Xavier Portraits*, Old Xaverians Association, Melbourne, 1993, p. 307.

> We would also like them to estimate the many failures of the Church to be faithful to her founder, with clarity, honesty, and an undisturbed spiritual poise.
>
> We want to help pupils to take the centre of gravity of their lives, the centre of their thinking and wishing, out of themselves, and replant it in God and their fellow human beings.

An essential part of a school's endeavors to change its clientele's expectations will often entail persuading them that the school exists to serve the wider community beyond its front gates. No school can truly call itself successful without a commitment to this ideal. A school's community service programs – sadly the term 'community service' has taken on punitive and disciplinary overtones in recent times – are critical for young people to stretch their hearts and empathize with those less fortunate and more needy than themselves. Even more important than the actual service activities is the reflection component to be integrated as an essential part of the program. If community service is to be more than an outpouring of well-intentioned activity, there must be some framework for students to reflect on their work and understand how it is affecting their hearts. Community service is about stretching the heart in empathy and compassion. Without a carefully structured device like journal-writing built into the program, this real purpose will be lost or diminished. Journals which focus on such basic questions as 'What did I learn during that experience?' or 'How did I feel in that situation? Why?' can help students get in touch with their hearts. Done well, writing is a powerful tool for surfacing one's real feelings.

Community service programs, planned thoughtfully and executed carefully, enable young people to understand the fundamental importance of building a just society. Indeed, the touchstone for establishing justice has always been the capacity to care for those least able to assert their rights: the widow, the orphan, and the stranger. Something of this is captured in the old Celtic verse:

I sought my God,
My God I could not see.
I sought my soul,
My soul eluded me.
I sought my brother,
And I found all three.

*Reflections**

The Global Community

'It takes a whole village to raise a child.' African Proverb

More than ever today it makes sense to talk about one global community. Let us not descend to the violence of terrorists who have no respect for human life. Rather let us remember that we are all connected, all linked across the world. Gerard Hughes said once, 'When a baby throws its rattle out of the cradle, the planets rock. We are miniscule parts of a vast interlocking system dancing through space, affecting and being affected by everything around us.'

Someone else said that dropping a stone in Sydney Harbour will have an effect, however small, on a whale in the Antarctic Ocean, even on a distant star. The poet Francis Thompson was absolutely right when he wrote in 'The Mistress of Vision':

All things by immortal power,
Near or far,
Hiddenly
To each other linked are,

---

* Please see the References, pp. 224-227, for full details for works cited in the 'Reflections' sections.

> Thou canst not stir a flower
> Without troubling a star.

School Assembly, 12 September 2001 (Australian EST time), shortly after the horrors of the terrorist attack on the World Trade Center in New York

No life without community

This week's College Musical, 'Anything Goes', is probably the biggest community-building exercise in the school's calendar. I had these things to say about it in the School Assembly on Wednesday:

'In the middle of the last century we saw our planet Earth from space for the first time. One of the first to see Earth from space later wrote: "When you look at the Earth from space … there are no national boundaries visible … It's a planet – all one place. All the beings on it are mutually dependent, like living on a lifeboat. Whatever the causes that divide us, the earth will be here a thousand – a million – years from now."'

Michael Jordan, the great basketball player, said once, 'There are plenty of teams in every sport that have great players and never win titles. Most of the time, those players aren't willing to sacrifice for the greater good of the team. The funny thing is, in the end, their unwillingness to sacrifice only makes individual goals more difficult to achieve … I'd rather have five guys with less talent who are willing to come together as a team than five guys who consider themselves stars and aren't willing to sacrifice. Talent wins games, but teamwork and intelligence win championships.'

T. S. Eliot wrote:

> What life have you if you have not life together?
> There is no life that is not in community,
> And no community not lived in praise of God.
> (Choruses from 'The Rock')

'Viewpoint', 9 March 2001

Parents and teachers working together

I dreamed I stood in a studio
And watched two sculptors there.
The clay they used was a young child's mind
And they fashioned it with care.
One was a teacher: the tools she used
Were books and music and art.
The other a parent with a guiding hand
And a gentle, loving heart.
Day after day the teacher toiled
With touch that was deft and sure,
While the parent labored just as hard
And polished and smoothed it o'er.
When at last their task was done,
They were proud of what they had wrought.
For the things they had moulded into the child
Could neither be sold nor bought.
And both agreed they would have failed
If they had worked alone;
For behind the parents stood the school
And behind the teacher, the home.

Author unknown

The kitchen table

There are lots of things wrong with Australia today,
And I'd like to have something to say if I may.
You know that, forsooth, our problem with youth,
Untidy, ill-mannered, untamed and uncouth,
Is the fact that their home life is so often unstable
And it's all for the lack of a kitchen table.

Remember how once we would sit down as one,
And Dad would say grace when the carving was done.
Our own serviettes from our own special rings,
And we all knew our manners and etiquette things.
Then our elders would tell us of custom and fable,
When we all sat about at our kitchen table.

Now they're building new mansions with four-car garages.
Our working lives mortgaged to interest and charges.
There's less time at home for the tea to be made,
And it's seldom today that a table is laid.
There's room after room under gable and gable,
But there's not enough room for a kitchen table.

At weekends the parents are chauffeurs unpaid,
No wonder they're tired and their tempers are frayed,
As they ferry their broods to arenas of sport,
Where the culture of winning's intensively taught.
And there's more on the tele both free and by cable,
So there's no room for talk around the kitchen table.

Karl Marx called religion the drug of the people,
But there's scant regard now for the church or the steeple.
Just give 'em more sport and don't let 'em think,
And keep 'em away from the kitchen sink.
We'll give 'em more sport and the culture of Babel,
The throwaway culture that threw out the table.

With the culture of rap and their baseball caps,
There'll soon be no fellers, no blokes and no chaps.
When they all dress the same then it's little surprise
That the girls swear as much and as foul as the guys.
So we grandparents must, just as long as we're able,
Keep our culture alive round the kitchen table.

Richard Magoffin OAM, June 1999

A vision for community

Then, in my dreams of the Last Day,
Our Lord will come back and reward us for having,
by his grace,
straightened the world out,
and having the poor competent and the rich thoughtful
and the well-protected kindly and generous and
involved, and the educated enthralled with
the kingdom of God, and the spiritual able to
perceive him in such a way as to make him visible to us.

These are the words of a Jesuit priest who died in a very poor, black area of Washington DC, where he gained a wonderful reputation for creating shelters for the homeless, providing meals and medical, dental and legal help. Among his papers after his death at age 80 was found this note which he had written to himself. It sums up well our hopes for all students being informed, being involved and making a difference.

Serving the community around us

I know you think you should make a trip to Calcutta, but I strongly advise you to save your airfare and spend it on the poor in your own country. It's easy to love people far away. It's not always easy to love those who live right next to us. There are thousands of people dying for a bit of bread, but there are thousands more dying for a bit of love or a bit of acknowledgement. The truth is that the worst disease today is not leprosy or tuberculosis; it's being unwanted, it's being left out, it's being forgotten.
Mother Teresa

> God give me the strength
> to look up and not down,
> to look forward and not back,
> to look out and not in, and
> to lend a hand.
> Edward Everett Hale

A Year 11 student on community

I quote the following letter in full because it captures so well the importance of community service in forming our students. It was written in August 2001 by a Year 11 boarder. He was also a member of the Year 11 Arrupe Academy Leadership program. He is speaking of his experience of working in the Cana Communities which serve homeless people in inner Sydney.

Dear Fr Gleeson,

Mr Hogan on Wednesday at School Assembly asked for help with several shelters run by Cana Communities. During the first week of the holidays, I spent thirty hours working at these shelters helping out around the place or just talking to the people.

The idea of Cana Communities is to give those people who are not accepted by society, for whatever reason, a place where they can feel part of a community. It comes back to that idea that many of the boys raised about not feeling comfortable with homeless people, often having apprehensions about talking to or even approaching them. These feelings separate the underprivileged from the privileged, hence the need for a community where they feel they belong. During my time at Cana I worked at three different places: De Porres House, Teresa House and Cana Cafeteria. From cleaning toilets, to cooking dinner to sleeping over at the hostel I was never short of experiences.

But how did these thirty hours touch my life? After careful thought I think I can narrow it down to three main ways:

1. It made me appreciate my life more. This seemed a common theme from the speakers, but nonetheless I believe it is still an important one. Such experiences of community education as my one, in a way, provide a safety net when things are blue. Many mornings I might wake up and be panicking at the thought of a test or complaining that there is no hot water in the Division, but, by being educated through my experience at Cana, I am able to step back, take a look at the Big Picture and appreciate what God has given me and how I can use these gifts for the Greater Good. I can pick myself up and face the day and the world with a whole new attitude.

2. It eliminated that fear of difference. It is common throughout all societies that the majority are not fond of difference, and this is also the case in the streets of Sydney. Many rich business men/women walk past the underprivileged each day and probably think to themselves, 'Why is it my problem. They probably got themselves there in the first place – they don't deserve help.' But my experience demonstrated to me that these people are just as much my neighbour as you, my friends or the Pope. I was, personally, brought up in a very sanitized environment where I was not even to look at 'those people'. I met one man, David, who was an excellent poet. Probably he, on his own, in one hour eliminated my ignorance and fear of difference.

3. Finally, and probably most importantly, it instilled in me a greater love of generosity. It might sound a bit cliched but it is true. As Daniel Street was saying, when he came back from his Grummit Scholarship he felt empty because he was not doing something for the community. I now feel the same way. I now look forward to every second Sunday where I go out to Redfern and talk to the homeless and addicted. (One word of advice that I would have liked to give the guys would have been to dive in the deep end. I have done other community service for DEAS in the past and have enjoyed it, but not really loved it. By diving in the deep end of society and really seeing how much there is to be done you realize that you can make more of a difference than just delivering newspapers.) By really jumping into your community service you begin to love the feeling that comes over you when you see that disabled man smiling and you know that you have made his day.

My service was an experience to say the least. To conclude, here is a quote that was hanging on Fr Stoney's door that really touched me:

> There are those who give with joy, and that joy is their reward.
> And there are those who give with pain, and that pain is their baptism.
> And there are those who give and know not pain in giving,
> nor do they seek joy, nor give with mindfulness of virtue;
> They give as in yonder valley the myrtle breathes its fragrance into space.
> Through the hands of such as these God speaks, and from
> behind their eyes
> He smiles upon the earth (Kahlil Gibran, *The Prophet*).

Thank you, Father, for allowing me to express my feelings about my experiences of Community Education. This letter makes me feel that I have put my two bob's worth in, which is important to me. I commend you on running an excellent Academy and I look forward to the next one.

Keep keeping human rights on the front page

I understand that not everyone agrees with what I write in 'Viewpoint' but I take great heart from the Riverview mother who wrote to me in 2002 saying that she sent her son to a Jesuit school 'partly because I have been a bit of an intellectual snob and because the Jesuits (in my experience and reading) stood out as speaking for those who could not do so for themselves … Keep keeping human rights on the front page.' I have the author's permission to quote here another fine letter received from a Riverview parent last weekend. While I have protected the family's identity, the message remains very powerful.

My Dear Father Gleeson

I am writing this letter at the insistance of my son. He tells me that 'some parents' are unhappy about your comments (made in your columns in 'Viewpoint' as well as, presumably, in your talks to students), on the so-called 'asylum seeker issue'. Apparently, these parents feel that it is a 'political' issue and as such you have no business expressing your opinion on it. He feels strongly that the Catholic Church in general and the Jesuits in particular have a definite role in 'social justice' issues. He feels that although such issues have 'political' ramifications, the Jesuits should not shy away from stating their position, even if such action is deemed 'controversial'. My wife and I said we totally agreed with his views on this matter. He said that if that were so, we should write and support your position. Hence, this note.

I come from the so-called 'Third World'. I came to Australia as a 'legitimate' migrant, having obtained the necessary visas, etc. However, when I walk down the street I look no different from 'those people', as the latest bunch of asylum seekers are contemptuously referred to. Whenever I think of them I merely say to myself, '… There but for the grace of God go I.'

While it is heartening that a number of influential Australians have spoken up for these hapless people, it saddens me that many powerful politicians and commentators have succeeded in persuading the vast majority of 'White' Australians that 'these people' are 'dangerous', 'devious' and not worthy of our sympathy.

I belong to a microscopic minority within the Riverview Community. My support for what is obviously your 'minority view' may not amount to much. What heartens me is that you have instilled in my son the value of social justice. Being from an 'ethnic minority' himself, it is probably easier for him to accept your point of view in support of another minority. What will be remarkable is if you manage to persuade the 'White' kids that it is indeed Christian to speak up for social justice, however, unpopular, 'controversial' or 'political' it may be.

'Viewpoint', 9 August 2002

You are not alone

This was the theme of the following letter written by a parent in response to the above letter from 'a microscopic minority' at the College.

Dear Father Gleeson,

The letter you quote from a parent about the asylum seekers issue saddens me, as the parent believes that in voicing support for a more humanitarian response to asylum seekers he is part of 'a microscopic minority' at the College. He is not so alone as he imagines. We all share the shame that he perceives this to be the case. Hence my email, voicing support for a change of heart befitting a civilised nation, a much needed change, as signalled by yesterday's High Court decision. Jesuits engage with 'hot potatoes' and – this is our blessing – encourage our sons to do likewise. To be alive is to be political, unless one is mute. To be mute where we enjoy such freedom of speech is, I suggest, both irresponsible and un-Catholic.

Thank you for the holistic education you provide to our sons.

'Viewpoint', 16 August 2002

Human life as a spider web

The other day I read of human life described as a spider web:

'If you touch it anywhere, you set the whole thing trembling ... The life that I touch for good or ill will touch another life, and that in turn another, until who knows where the trembling stops or in what far place and time my touch will be felt. Our lives are linked. No man, no woman, is an island.'

The gift of friendship with others is contagious.

More on family meals together

A recent report from the United States claims that children who were expected to sit down with the rest of the family at meal times, and who were encouraged to talk at the table, were doing better at school, had higher self-esteem, better social competence, and had better prospects of getting a job.

This report confirms a study conducted 25 years ago in Melbourne, 'Talk Up at the Table'. The author, Don Edgar, foundation director of the Australian Institute of Family Studies (*EQ Australia*, Issue 1, Autumn 1998) had been looking for the correlates of adolescent competence: which kids with what sorts of parents were most likely to do well. He found that on almost every outcome measure – school results, self esteem, social competence, optimism versus pessimism, good parent-child relationships, an expectation of later success in life – the kids (whether rich or poor) who were allowed to chatter and exchange ideas at meal times scored significantly higher than those who were told to shut up and eat their meals.

At the time, he interpreted the meal talk factor as illustrative of an openness on the part of parents to the free expression of ideas, mutual respect within the family, and warmth and structure combining to give children a sense of place and security in their lives. The new US study renews his faith in the efficacy of eating together and letting the meal talk flow. It may be noisy, argumentative and hard to manage, with parents and young people working different hours, but its outcomes are worth the trouble. Pity the poor family that never cooks its own meals, never sits at the one table, never has to cope with the noisy conflict of everyone wanting to talk at once.

A Family

A family is a place
to cry and laugh
and vent frustration,
to ask for help
and tease and yell,
to be touched and
hugged and smiled at.
A family is people
who care when you are sad,
who love you no matter what,
who share your triumphs,
who don't expect you to be perfect,
just growing with honesty in your own decisions.
A family is a circle
where we learn to make good decisions,
where we learn to think before we do,
where we learn integrity and table manners
and respect for other people;
where we are special,
where we listen and are listened to,
where we learn the rules of life
to prepare ourselves for the world.
The world is a place where anything can happen:
if we grow up in a loving family we are ready
    for the world.

Lessons from Geese

1. As each bird flaps its wings, it creates an 'uplift' for the bird following. By flying in a 'V' formation the flock adds 71 per cent greater flying range than if the bird flew alone.

Lesson: People who share a common direction and sense of community can get where they are going more quickly and more easily because they are traveling on the thrust of one another.

2. Whenever a goose falls out of formation, it suddenly feels the drag and resistance of trying to fly alone, and quickly gets back into formation to take advantage of the 'lifting power' of the bird immediately in front.

Lesson: If we have as much sense as a goose, we will stay in formation with those who are headed where we want to go and be willing to accept their help as well as give ours to the others.

3. When the lead goose gets tired, it rotates back into the formation and another goose flies at the point position.

Lesson: It pays to take turns doing the hard tasks and share the leadership with people. As with geese, we are interdependent on each other.

4. The geese in formation 'honk' from behind to encourage those up front to keep up their speed.

Lesson: We need to make sure our 'honking' from behind is encouraging and not something else.

5. When a goose gets sick or wounded or shot down, two geese drop out of formation and follow it down to help and protect it. They stay with it until it is able to fly again or dies. Then they launch out on their own, with another formation, or catch up with the flock.

Lesson: If we have as much sense as geese, we too will stand by each other in difficult times as well as when we are strong.

from a speech by Angeles Arrien based on the work of Milton Olson

'For just as the body is one and has many members, and all the members of the body, though many are one body, so it is with Christ.'
1 Corinthians 12:12

Children learn what they live.
If a child lives with criticism,
He learns to condemn.
If a child lives with hostility,
He learns to fight.
If a child lives with ridicule,
He learns to be shy.
If a child lives with shame,
He learns to feel guilty.
If a child lives with tolerance,
He learns to be patient.
If a child lives with encouragement,
He learns confidence.
If a child lives with praise,
He learns to appreciate.
If a child lives with fairness,
He learns justice.
If a child lives with security,
He learns to have faith.
If a child lives with approval,
He learns to like himself.
If a child lives with acceptance and friendship,
He learns to find love in the world.

(The non-inclusive language indicates that this reflection comes from an older source.)

Family versus the cult of self

In this, the International Year of the Family (1994), we have heard all sorts of advice for parents and will continue to do so for the next few months. Indeed, one good way to deaden discussion on important topics is to devote an International Year to it. At the risk of initiating another turn-off at this point, I would like to share some thoughts from an article by Dr Don Edgar, formerly Director of the Australian Institute of Family Studies.

He reminds us firstly that children are essentially conservative. They need clear boundaries, firm guidelines, because they rely on stable arrangements to flourish.

Secondly, children need security, a sense of being safe. Fear that their parents may divorce is very real and children need reassurance either that everyday conflict is 'normal' and won't lead to family disruption, or that, once separated, they can still maintain a stable relationship with both parents.

Most importantly, children need time together with parents and family. On a recent trip to Armidale I was edified to meet a family who manage without a television set. They hire one for the children only during the school holidays. Clearly, the TV set and/or video recorder can fragment family life.

At a school like Riverview, the fourth maxim remains very dear to us: children need a set of values, beliefs. To feel part of something bigger than themselves is important for children. Don Edgar poses the following challenging question for all of us: 'How can we recapture that sense of being part of the civil society, where self-absorption is not the only ethic and where responsibility for others, a sense of being useful, of having a stake in what happens around us, becomes the starting point for self-esteem?'

Finally, we cannot remind ourselves often enough: children need example and action. Love shows itself in deeds, rather than words, as St Ignatius puts it in his *Spiritual Exercises*.

The Ignatian, April 1994

Making too much of self-esteem

The cult of self-development, or even a spiritual path that doesn't wake you up to do something about the painful realities of this world, can be just as narcissistic, just as entrapping. Stephen R. Covey, author of the hugely successful best-seller *The Seven Habits of Highly Effective People*, points out that 'Much of the self-esteem literature has created a kind of narcissism of taking care of the self, loving the self, and nurturing the self and has neglected the next step: service.' Challengingly, he asks, 'You may be good, but what are you good for?'

From Stephanie Dowrick, *Forgiveness and Other Acts of Love*, 1997

Men and women for others

Non nobis solum nati sumus. I thought our much-loved Father Pedro Arrupe had coined the expression 'Men for Others' in his famous 1973 address to European Jesuit Alumni/ae in Valencia. However, Jesuit historian Father John O'Malley has traced this term to a line from Cicero, beloved by Renaissance humanists, which the early Jesuits enjoyed quoting: *Non nobis solum nati sumus*: 'We are not born for ourselves alone.'

Star two

Living with our feet on the ground and our eyes on the stars

> *Late last fall, I sat with him on a bench outside the monastery and watched dazed yellow jackets crawl on the bits of apple we put on the ground. When the stars began to come out, he named them all his friends. He'd been a monk for more than fifty years and he said: 'Heaven's gonna be great. Do you know the best thing I ever did? I made a clock that keeps star-time.'*
> **Kathleen Norris**, *Dakota: A Spiritual Geography*,
> p. 125

In 1992, after eleven years in the saddle as Headmaster of Xavier College, Melbourne, my generous superiors gave me the opportunity to take some sabbatical leave. At beautiful Newman College attached to Melbourne University, armed with a new laptop computer, and with many fewer pastoral responsibilities I finally had some time to accept an invitation to write a book on teaching values. I planned initially to call the book 'Roots and Wings', resonating somewhat with the thinking of this Star Two. Regrettably, the publishers were shy about aligning their name to one of these words in the title – no prizes for guessing which word – so I had to look for something else. I eventually chose the words 'Striking a Balance,' because I wanted to convey the idea that all of us need to acquire the art of balancing and juggling if we are to hold together the various parts of our life.

When I was a student of theology in Melbourne in the 1970s, there was a marvellous character living with us named Brother Jim Madden. One of his favorite pastimes was juggling, and often after lunch he would go into the back garden and juggle three or four and sometimes more oranges for us students as his encouraging audience. He rarely dropped an orange – even at the age of seventy-something. He told me his secret was to concentrate on all the oranges in the air. As soon as you focused on just one and forgot the others, the whole lot would come down.

All of us are jugglers or balancers in life. Just to pick up this book and read parts of it will require readers to juggle their time to meet other competing demands on them. Like all balancers, we sometimes fall, but we should remember that, where we stumble, there we find our opportunity. With our feet firmly planted on the ground and our eyes on the stars, all of us are continually striving to balance – and by example, teach others to balance – values and freedom, rights and responsibilities, mind and heart, thinking and feeling, involvement and detachment, male and female, body and spirit, giving and receiving, inheritance and ownership, the formal and the intimate, the conservative and the innovative.

Where any of these elements are allowed to get out of balance, where we lose proper perspective, both suffer. To have enough is enough. For example, we have got ourselves into so much trouble in recent years by talking excessively about 'my' rights, without realizing that they make no sense if they are not balanced by my responsibilities. The simple truth of the matter is that, if I do not protect the rights of my neighbour, I will lose such rights for myself.

There is an old saying that the two most important things parents and teachers can give their children are roots and wings. In other words, young people need to learn that their freedom – their quest for the stars – is always limited by their responsibilities to those around them in the wider community. Freedom is a life-long goal to be achieved, never assumed. Freedom without responsibility, reaching for the stars without having a platform or springboard of obligation to others, is a nonsense. The two must go hand in hand at all times.

In this context I am reminded of writer Gore Vidal's words when speaking about young people and their loss of literature. He remarked that they 'are quite unable to comprehend the doubleness of things, the unexpected paradox, the sense of yes-no without which there can be no true intelligence, no means, in fact, of examining life as opposed to letting it wash over one.'[1]

Not so long ago I read that a deprived child can be defined tellingly as 'one whose parents have no expectations'.[2] Young people need to have clear boundaries. While they have a natural need for mastery of their world, without boundaries it can be too overwhelming and confusing. Much of the chaos endured by many families, quite needlessly, comes from a lack of authority in providing a sense of leadership, order and predictability. Children crave routine and ritual. A family with no parental authority is a leaderless group.

Freedom and responsibility go hand in glove with accountability. I can remember admiring a school principal a few years ago for having the courage to keep her word and cancel the graduation celebrations for some of her senior girls. Despite several clear warnings, they had defied school policy at that low point of the annual calendar, the end of formal classes, to drive to another school to 'celebrate' same by causing disruption. In the face of much opposition from parents, the principal said simply that 'the girls must learn that actions have consequences'. The threatened punishment became reality.

As far back as 1982, Associate Professor Maurice Balson of Monash University wrote in an HBA Symposium paper: 'Consequences encourage individuals to develop more acceptable ways of behaving by allowing

---

[1] Gore Vidal, *Two Sisters*, Boston, Little, Brown, 1970, p. 41.
[2] Linda Kavelin Popov, Dan Popov, John Kavelin, *The Virtues Guide: A Handbook for Parents Teaching Virtues*, The Virtues Project, 1995, p. 4.

them to experience the consequences of their own behavior. The child who refuses to get up in the morning experiences the consequences of his or her lateness at school. A lunch left at home stays at home. Library books not returned prevent borrowing for a time. Property damaged by an individual is restored by that individual.'

We are what we do repeatedly. Excellence, then, is not an act but a habit. There is a fine balance to be achieved here by parents and teachers, indeed by all those who are forming the hearts and minds of our young people. On the one hand we want those in our care to be well grounded and to understand that there must be reasonable and balanced limits for responsible behavior. On the other hand, we want them also to reach for the stars, to be adventuresome and dream about achievement of the highest order, to strive for excellence in all their pursuits. 'Of barriers to be broken down, the hardest, most important one is undoubtedly mediocrity.'[3]

In all this reaching for the stars, the role of the imagination is crucial. The very popoular US writer, Thomas Moore claims that 'we are condemned to live out what we cannot imagine.'[4] Through the imagination, Kathleen Fischer observes, a person 'reconstructs past experience and is able to give a verdict on his or her self and life.'[5] Telling our story, particularly in the presence of a careful listener, will reveal those images responsible for attitudes of discouragement and confusion, or emotions of fear, depression and resentment. It will help us find a sequence and pattern in our life: to order events is itself an act of judgment. In all stories there are 'discoveries, revelations, and surprises in the telling: gifts of grace now forgotten, wounds not yet healed, goals and desires persisting over many years.'[6] Stories are clearly an important avenue to developing the life of the imagination.

---

[3] Dom Helder Camara, *A Thousand Reasons for Living*, DLT, London, 1984, p. 79.
[4] Thomas Moore, *Care of the Soul*, p. 224.
[5] Kathleen R. Fischer, *The Inner Rainbow: The Imagination in Christian Life*, Paulist Press, New Jersey, 1981, p. 102.

During her highly successful national radio program of interviews over eight years, 'The Search for Meaning', Caroline Jones came to the recognition 'that a person's experience, their story, is sacred ground, that it's essential to them, that they're lost without it, that it needs to be told, and, importantly, to be heard'.[7] Every story demands a listener, and to listen to a person's story and understand the unexpressed questions and yearnings contained therein, requires that we believe in the uniqueness and importance of each story, of each individual life. Many young people, however, are afraid to tell their story because they think that it is neither clever nor beautiful. No one would want to hear it. Because storytelling is an excellent way of caring for the soul, we must find ways of slicing through this natural reluctance to tell one's story.

All of us dealing with young people are in competition for their hearts with a variety of image-makers in the rock world and consumer society. We have to capture their imaginations. If Irish Jesuit author Michael Paul Gallagher is right, that, 'apathy is often the face of hurt hope, or hidden hunger,'[8] then it is our task to provide better images of hope for our young people. How can we do that?

Psychologist Charles Shelton, in his excellent book, *Morality and the Adolescent*, argues that adults ministering to young people must help them 'frame' their decisions and choices. He uses the word 'frame' deliberately, because he believes it is the adult's task to provide images or pictures to assist the young person in the decision-making process.

Just as pictures have frames to heighten imaginative immediacy and intensify emotional identification, so too we teachers and parents must help young people 'frame' the pictures that fire their imaginations. After all, the imagination provides adolescents with another way of see-

---

[6] ibid., p. 105.
[7] Caroline Jones, *The Search For Meaning Collection*, ABC Books, Sydney, 1995, p. xi.
[8] Michael Paul Gallagher, *Struggles of Faith*, The Columba Press, Dublin, 1991, p. 78.

ing themselves and their world. It is a route to their hearts, their deeper selves. While the examples used by Shelton refer to the moral decision-making process, they can be adapted, I am sure, for use in all situations:

> Having adolescents dream of who they are becoming, and reflecting on the values present in this process.
>
> Having young people imagine a perfect world and what it would be like, and exploring with them their own role in forming and helping to build such a world.
>
> Having them reflect on just one 'day' – on all that has happened, sorting out the unexpected and grateful moments. Preoccupied as they are with the immediate, they often tend to forget or take for granted the recognition they have received from others – even a smile from a friend.
>
> Having adolescents imagining themselves as a gift or a present to someone. They then describe the gift. What does the gift say about the young giver?[9]

All of this technique proposed by Shelton is grounded in the belief that 'imagining things being otherwise may be a first step toward acting on the belief that they can be changed.'[10]

Surprisingly, it was Adolf Hitler who once exclaimed:

> When all's said, we should be grateful to the Jesuits. Who knows if, but for them, we might have abandoned the Gothic architecture for the light, airy, bright architecture of the Counter-Reformation. In the face of Luther's efforts to lead an upper clergy, which had acquired profane habits, back to mysticism, the Jesuits restored to the world the joy of the senses.

That phrase – 'the joy of the senses' – reminds us all of the central

---

[9] Charles M. Shelton, *Morality and the Adolescent: A Pastoral Psychology Approach*, Crossroad, New York, 1989, pp. 145, 146.

[10] Maxine Greene, *Releasing the Imagination: Essays on Education, Arts and Social Change*, Jossey-Bass, San Francisco, 1995, p. 22.

place the arts should have in our school curricula. Music, dance performances, art exhibitions, concerts, stories, poems, plays, films – all have the unique power to release the imagination. For the 'role of imagination is not to resolve, not to point the way, not to improve. It is to awaken, to disclose the ordinarily unseen, unheard, and unexpected.'[11]

Kathleen Fischer refers to the imagination as our inner rainbow. In linking the skies with the earth, imagination enables us to dream, to wonder, and to reach for the sky from a standpoint firmly planted on the ground.

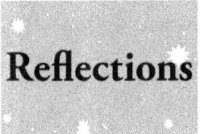

Reflections

God could not be everywhere so He created Mothers.
Talmud

Balance

Dear God,
　　We pray for balance and exchange. Balance us like trees. As the roots of a tree shall equal its branches so must the inner life be equal to the outer life. And as the leaves shall nourish the roots so shall the roots give nourishment to the leaves. Without equality and exchange of nourishment there can be no growth and no love. Amen.
　　Michael Leunig, *A Common Prayer*, Collins Dove, 1991

Be an owner, not a blamer

Owners take full responsibility for all their actions and even their emotional responses. Blamers shift the responsibility on to others – either people or things. Owners get to know themselves because they are in contact with

---

[11] Maxine Greene, *Releasing the Imagination*, Wiley, 1995, p. 28.

their own inner workings. Blamers never get to know themselves because they live in a world of denial, and unreal world.

Often the difference between being an owner and a blamer can be recognized in our language patterns. An owner uses the phrase, 'I've decided to …'; a blamer the phrase 'I have to …' Learn to take responsibility for who you are.

Inform, no. 15, Catholic Adult Education Centre, Sydney

Life lived generously in the service of others

Rights and responsibilities are of a piece. In this context, I was struck by what a Boston University Professor, Kevin Ryan, had to say about responsibility in the following story:

'Louis Slottin was a physicist in Los Alamos on the Manhattan Project that led to the development of the atomic bomb. One day in 1946, he was working with his team on a critical experiment that required assembling pieces of plutonium. With minute movements, he was nudging pieces of plutonium toward one another trying to form a mass of plutonium large enough to produce a chain reaction.

'Through his own error, he made a critical mistake and moved two pieces too close together. A chain reaction began and alarms went off as the room was filled with radioactivity. Without a moment's hesitation, Slottin reached in and pulled the pieces apart with his bare hands. In the blink of an eye he had signed his own death certificate, since he had exposed himself to a large dose of radioactivity. He then calmly turned to his seven coworkers and told them to mark precisely their position during the accident so that their degree of exposure to radioactivity could be determined. He then apologized to them and predicted what would turn out to be exactly true: he would die, and they would survive.

'Slottin's heroic act did not just happen. It was the result of a life lived devoted to the enduring habit of responsibility.

'Responsibility is the quality of realizing and acting upon our obligations; obligations to those with whom we are connected. We are not born with responsibility. We can't buy it. We can't buy quickie self-help courses in it. It is, however, essential to a civilized and democratic community.'

Louis Slottin's life was described by Professor Ryan as 'a life lived devoted to the enduring habit of responsibility'. What a splendid description of a 'man for others'. It is very similar to what Father Bill Byron sj said to us at the World Congress of Jesuit Alumni/ae at Riverview in 1997 – that 'life is lived well only when it is lived generously in the service of others.' An old African proverb advises that 'God gives nothing to those who keep their arms crossed.'

Speech Day Address, December 1998

The power of the imagination

The way we habitually imagine ourselves, our fellow men and what we call God is one of the most formative factors in life. Let anyone picture in his or her imagination the kind of person they long to be, and view that picture frequently and steadily enough, and they will be drawn towards it. Within the imagination resides much of the power to control our health, achieve our goals and develop our characters.

Christ knew the power of a fired imagination to motivate people. He enrolled as learners a group of individuals whose horizons were bounded by a country lake. He led them to visualize themselves as the salt of the earth and the light of the world. He filled their imaginations with pictures of themselves carrying his message to 'the uttermost parts of the earth'.

The Age, 'Saturday Reflection', 10 August 1985

Embracing paradox

The following piece is understandably sombre. It was written by an American student at Columbine High School when school reopened in 2000 after the horrendous massacre of the previous year.

> The paradox of our time in history is that:
> We have taller buildings, but shorter tempers;
> Wider freeways, but narrower viewpoints.

We spend more, but have less,
We buy more, but enjoy it less.

We have bigger houses and smaller families.
More conveniences but less time.
We have more degrees, but less sense.
More knowledge, but less judgment,
More experts, but more problems,
More medicine but less wellness.
We drink too much, smoke too much,
Laugh too little, drive too fast, get angry too quickly,
stay up too late, get up too tired, read too seldom,
watch TV too much.

We have multiplied our possessions, but reduced our values.
We talk too much, love too seldom, and hate too often.

We've learned how to make a living, but not a life;
We've added years to life, not life to years.

We've been all the way to the moon and back,
But have trouble crossing the street to meet the new neighbour.

We've conquered outer space, but not inner space.
We've done larger things, but not better things.
We've cleaned up the air, but polluted the soul.

We plan more, but accomplish less.
We've learned to rush, but not to wait.

We build more computers to hold more information to produce more copies than ever, but have less communication.

These are the times of fast foods and slow digestion, tall men, shorter character;
Steep profits, and shallow relationships.

These are the times of world peace but domestic warfare.

More leisure, but less fun;
More kinds of food, but less nutrition.

These are the days of two incomes, but more divorce;
Of fancier houses, but broken homes.
Disposable diapers, throw-away morality,
One-night stands,
And pills that do everything from cheer to quiet to kill.

It is a time when there is much in the shop window,
And nothing in the stockroom;
A time when technology can bring this letter to you,
And a time when you can choose either to share this insight,
or just to DELETE.

On excellence

If a man is called to be a street sweeper,
He should sweep streets as
Michelangelo painted, or
Beethoven composed music, or
Shakespeare wrote poetry.
He should sweep streets so well that
all the hosts of heaven and earth
will pause to say, here lived a
great street sweeper who did
his job well.
Martin Luther King Jr

Unique and special

I'm special.
In all the world there's nobody like me. Since the beginning of time, there has never been another person like me.

Nobody has my smile. Nobody has my eyes, my nose, my hair, my voice. I'm special.

No one can be found who has my handwriting. Nobody anywhere has my tastes – for food or music or art. No one sees things just as I do.
In all of time there's been no one who laughs like me, no one who cries like me. And what makes me laugh and cry will never provoke identical laughter and tears from anybody else, ever.
No one reacts to any situation just as I would react. I'm special.

I am the only one in all of creation who has my set of abilities. Oh, there will always be somebody who is better at one of the things I am good at, but no one in the universe can reach the quality of my combination of talents, ideas, abilities, and feelings. Like a room full of musical instruments, some may excel alone, but none can match the symphony sound when all are played together. I am a symphony.

I am special, and I am beginning to realize it is no accident that I am special. I am beginning to see that God made me special. I am beginning to see that God made me special for a very special purpose. He must have a job for me that no one else can do as well as I. Out of all the billions of applicants, only one is qualified, only one has the right combination of what it takes.

The one is me, because …
        I'm special.

Anonymous

Imagination – the treasure

Formal education has enormous potential to source this precious asset of imagination. Calling on the power of the microscope, breaking open the text of a Shakespearean play, accessing the thoughts and feelings of another culture/language are just a few of the possibilities open to educators in this area of the imagination. One of the most powerful examples in my own experience was to set for study by my Year 12 Literature class a slim volume of three plays by Athol Fugard, a South African playwright.

The plays dealt variously with the passbook situation, (in 'Sizwe Bansi is Dead') the prison experience, (in 'The Island') and the infamous Immorality Act outlawing sexual relationships between blacks and other racial groups. None of us in that class would ever be able to experience personally what it was to be black and living under apartheid. But I can guarantee that these plays left an indelible impression and a level of understanding in those girls that no amount of political comment could match.

By calling on the imagination, literature offers the opportunity of vicarious experience – maybe life at one remove but definitely life and to a depth unimagined.

Deirdre Rofe, Jesuit Lenten Seminar Talk, 1998

Longing to grow

> A passionate longing to grow, to become, is what we need.
> There can be no place for the anaemic in spirit,
> the sceptics, the pessimists, the sad of heart,
> the weary, the immobilists.
> Life is ceaseless discovery
> Life is movement.

Pierre Teilhard de Chardin

Blooming – in your own time

Once upon a time there was a spring season when the jonquils popped out of the ground and, as usual, bloomed before all the other flowers. But this year they made fun of the other flowers which were just beginning to send their green shoots into the air.

'Look at us with our golden blooms!' yelled the jonquils. 'You tulips and iris and chrysanthemums are nothing. We have beautiful blossoms and you are just some insignificant foliage!'

But one day the jonquils lost their blooms, just about the time the tulips were beginning to flower. The tulips, having had their fill of all the bragging done by the jonquils, had to have their say. So they did the same thing to the other flowers.

'Look at the glory of our colours', they said to the other flowers. 'You can't do this. You are nothing.'

At the end of the summer the chrysanthemums made their fantastic appearance with amazing colours. They screamed at what was left of the other plants. 'You are nothing but has-beens. We are the greatest.'

Of course, flowers do not do this, but we as human beings do it all the time. People are like flowers. Some bloom early and some bloom late, yet our culture wants everyone to bloom at the same time. It expects that at a certain age all must think and act like a given norm. All five-year-olds or all seventy-five-year-olds must conform to the same textbook image. We have not learned the lesson of the flowers.

It's not very appropriate for those who are in bloom to criticize those who are not. Nor does it do any good to scoff at those who no longer can show the talent and the beauty of another time. The greenery of the plants has its own majestic beauty even when there is no flower.

God gives individual gifts, and at different times, to each of us. This is the way we see his creation. If all the flowers were identical and they bloomed at the same time, it would be a dull world.

So it is with people.

Source unknown

Releasing the angel

One day a man came upon Michelangelo as he was chipping away with his chisel at a huge shapeless block of marble. He was surrounded by dust and fragments of marble. It was not a pretty sight.

The man asked Michelangelo what he was doing, and he replied, 'I'm releasing the angel imprisoned in this marble'.

A key aspect of education is to help free each person. To give each individual the care, skills and tools to try and achieve one's potential. To truly own one's gifts, qualities and talents. This can only be chiselled out by people with vision, love and the gift to educate, to bring out, to free.

Mario Bugna sj, Chaplain at Burke Hall,
Xavier Preparatory School, Melbourne

God speaks into the story

If human hope is like a bird in flight
then story is the air. It's where we live.

Story fuels the fires of the mind
for when we find our theme, we find ourselves.

It is God who speaks into the story of our lives
for God is the meaning maker of the world.

Rod Cameron osa, 'The Australian Experience of the Sacred', *Alcheringa*, p. 30

A failure of imagination?

I remember that great Benedictine nun, Joan Chittister, writing: 'Imagination asks "what's possible?"; technology asks "what works?"' It came to mind during the week when I heard someone saying that they were tired of all this talk on refugees. I am sure the same comment would have been made about issues of reconciliation. To be tired of these questions is to demonstrate a failure of imagination. After all, imagination is the eye of the soul, and questions of national hospitality and reconciliation are very much questions of healing our national soul. As Thomas Moore has said so powerfully in *Care of the Soul*, we are condemned to live out what we cannot imagine ...

Let me end with Joan Chittister again: 'Imagination breaks open the human mind to what is desirable when what is real is unbearable' (*Living Well*, p. 14).

'Viewpoint', 20 September 2002

Living is 90 per cent attitude

You will shine in the world like bright stars because you are offering it the word of life.

Philippians 2:15

It was journalist Phillip Adams who commented once that 'many words die of old age, while others expire through misuse. But more and more language shrivels through neglect.'[1] Something of this has happened to the word 'attitude', now that it has taken on a negative meaning to describe someone who is deemed to have 'attitude'. For me it has always been a strong word, full of energy, helping to describe people with positive qualities.

Perhaps it takes adversity to demonstrate a person's true strength of attitude. I remember in 1982 Archbishop Dominic Tang sj visiting us at a Xavier College School Assembly in Melbourne. In his broken but clear English, he told the story of how he was arrested, handcuffed, fingerprinted, photographed, and treated like a common criminal on 5 February 1958. The government charged him with being 'the most faithful running-dog of the reactionary Vatican'. He stayed in jail for 22 years until his sudden release in 1981 when he was given permission to leave China for a cancer operation in Hong Kong.

---

[1] Phillip Adams, 'The End of the Words Is Nigh', in *The Weekend Australian*, July 27-28, 1991.

He described how the years of incarceration consisted of long periods of interrogation, permanent intense hunger and malnutrition, and seven years of solitary confinement, where the only person he saw was the jailer bringing his food and the only literature to read was Communist propaganda. He was not allowed to receive letters, and was not given clothing or basic supplies. After his only pair of shoes wore out, he went barefoot for the rest of his time there.

One could have heard a pin drop that morning in the Great Hall, as staff and students alike listened in awe to his story of courage and perseverance, entirely without bitterness or resentment.

Some 12 years later, I was having breakfast in the dining room at the Jesuit High School in Hong Kong, when this same Dominic Tang asked if he could join me for the meal. It was shortly before he died at age 87, and I remember what a privilege it was to sit alongside him and recall his visit to Melbourne over a decade before.

Later I had the chance to read something of his philosophy in his autobiography on the web:

> In prison, I always asked God to grant me the grace to progress in virtue, for example, humility and obedience ... I obeyed only the regulations which did not conflict with the principles of my faith. I want to be gentle and kind to others, without resisting ill-treatment from others; when controlled and walked on, I did not complain. There are many opportunities for practising virtue in prison ... When I was a seminarian, I learned to do God's will. God's will required me to practise virtue in prison. This was God's love for me.

Dominic Tang was living evidence of Viktor Frankl's maxim that 'Those who have a "why" to live can bear with almost any "how".' His is a story of the most wonderful attitude.

As a professional and prolific scavenger of others' insights and ideas,

I have often used the following anonymous quotation pilfered from a Jesuit parish newsletter. It forms the basis for the rationale of this chapter.

> The longer I live, I realize the impact of attitude in life. Attitude to me is more important than fact. It is more important than the past, than education, than money, than circumstances, than failures, than success, than what other people think or say or do. It is more important than appearance, giftedness, or skill. It will make or break a company, a church, a home.
>
> The remarkable thing is that we have a choice every day regarding the attitude we will embrace for that day. We cannot change our past, we cannot change the fact that people will act in a certain way. We cannot change the inevitable. The only thing we can do is play on the one string we have, and that is our attitude.
>
> I am convinced that life is ten per cent of what happens to me and 90 per cent of how I react to it. And so it is with you.
>
> You are in charge of your attitude.

Another act of pilfering, this time from a Loreto school newsletter, brought the following reward:

> We are just like a person who stands between a mountain and the sea. In order to face the sea one turns one's back on the mountain. In order to face the mountain one must turn one's back on the sea. It is all a question of where we are facing and what we emphasize. Do we place the emphasis on what we are turning towards?

For Christians, there is a very close link between our attitude and the notion of conversion. Faith is, after all, essentially a matter of facing in the right direction. Sadly, we are often pointing ourselves in the wrong direction in life and inclined to pursue goals that are self-destructive or even destructive of others. Conversion is that invitation to make a turnaround, to realign our attitudes, to turn away from illusion and turn to reality.

When collating this material for publication, I was interested to see how much of it I had placed under the category of 'attitude'. This 'star' contained the majority of entries by a significant margin. There should be no surprise here. After all, what could be more fundamental than the way we see the world, our inclinations and orientations in life, our approach to and standpoint on important matters, what gets us out of bed in the morning and drives us to do what we do? All of these elements are part of our basic attitude to life.

> Nothing is more practical than finding God, that is,
> than falling in love in a quite absolute, final way.
> What you are in love with,
> what seizes your imagination,
> will affect everything.
> It will decide what will get you out of bed in the morning,
> what you will do with your evenings,
> how you spend your weekends,
> what you read,
> what you know that breaks your heart,
> and what amazes you with joy and gratitude.
> Fall in love, stay in love, and it will decide everything.
>
> Fr Pedro Arrupe SJ, General of the Society of Jesus, 1965–1983

It is noteworthy that this same Pedro Arrupe, as a missionary in Japan in 1942, was imprisoned in Yamaguchi for suspected espionage. While he was incarcerated for a brief period only, he wrote of his experience: 'Many were the things I learned during this time: the science of silence, of solitude, of severe and austere poverty, of inner dialogue with the "guest of my soul". I believe this was the most instructive month of my entire life.' On his release he remarked to the prison governor: 'I am not resentful towards you. You are someone who has done me good … you have taught me to suffer.'

Adversity seems to have a particular sweetness of challenge for people of attitude like Pedro Arrupe. The same is certainly true of another hero of mine – Nelson Mandela. That he should spend even longer in prison than Archbishop Tang – 27 years or nearly 10,000 days – to gain freedom for his people, prior to becoming the inaugural black president of South Africa, is truly remarkable. That he should emerge, like Archbishop Tang, from the austerities of this confinement without resentment and bitterness over this injustice points to the strength of his attitude. The following beautiful words testify to this. They are often attributed to Nelson Mandela's first speech as president but are actually from US author Marianne Williamson:[2]

> Our deepest fear is not that we are inadequate.
> Our deepest fear is that we are powerful beyond measure.
> It is our light, not our darkness, that most frightens us.
> We ask ourselves,
> who am I to be brilliant, gorgeous, talented, fabulous?
>
> Actually, who are you *not* to be?
> You are a child of God.
> Your playing small doesn't serve the world.
> There's nothing enlightened about shrinking
> so that other people won't feel insecure around you.
>
> We are all meant to shine, as children do.
> We were born to make manifest
> the glory of God that is within us.
> It's not just in some of us; it's in everyone,
> and as we let our own light shine,
> we unconsciously give other people
> permission to do the same.
> As we are liberated from our own fear,
> our presence automatically liberates others.

A similar strength can be found in the true story of Martin Gray,

---

[2] Marianne Williamson, *A Return to Love: Reflections on the Principles of 'A Course on Miracles'*, HarperCollins, New York, 1992, p. 190.

a survivor of the horrors of a concentration camp during the Second World War. How often it happens that stories of light and hope emerge from situations of darkness and despair!

After rebuilding his life and setting up a successful business, Gray married and raised a family. One day his wife and children were all killed when a forest fire destroyed their house in the south of France. His whole reason for living had been taken from him. Friends exhorted him to demand an inquiry into the causes of the fire, but Gray refused. Instead, he decided to place all his money into a new movement to protect nature from forest fires. Why? Gray explained that holding an inquiry was to wallow in the past and focus on issues of pain and blame. He preferred to give his energies to the future, to issues of life and growth. After all, life must be lived for, not against, someone or something.

A very important ingredient in attitude relates to the priority of being over doing. Author Robert Fulghum captures this well when talking about his new business card:

> What counts is not what I do, but how I think about myself while I'm doing it. In truth, I have a business card now. Finally figured out what to put on it. One word. 'Fulghum'. That's my occupation. And when I give it away, it leads to fine conversations.
>
> What I do is to be the best Fulghum I can be. Which means being a son, father, husband, friend, singer, dancer, eater, breather, sleeper, runner, walker, artist, writer, painter, teacher, preacher, citizen, poet, counselor, neighbor, dreamer, wisher, laugher, traveler, pilgrim, and on and on.
>
> I and you – we are infinite, rich, large, contradictory, living, breathing miracles – free human beings, children of God in the everlasting universe. That's what we do.[3]

I can recall journalist Caroline Jones making a similar point when

---

[3] Robert Fulghum, *It Was On Fire When I Lay Down On It*, Grafton, London, 1990, p. 70.

talking at a pastoral care conference about the great Australian Olympic sprinter, Betty Cuthbert:

> I was at a gathering the other evening where Betty Cuthbert was. She was one of my 'pin-up' girls as I was growing up. Do you remember our wonderful Olympic athlete: she was speed and elegance personified. And today she lives in a wheelchair and all that swiftness has been reduced to stillness.
>
> And, like everybody else, I was queuing up to see her. I wanted to spend a few seconds with Betty and just to be in her presence for thirty seconds was wonderfully life giving. All that 'doing' has been taken away and yet the radiance of her 'being' is infectious, beautiful.
>
> I talked to her a little bit. She said, 'I believe you've got the faith in recent years.' So I told her what I could about my rediscovery of the faith of my childhood. 'Oh well', she said, 'I've been born again, praise the Lord.' And she was full of the joy of living.
>
> I thought what a powerful thing she's teaching as she just sits immobile in that wheelchair with that extraordinary radiance on her face. I think she's teaching that when all our doing is taken away by illness, or losing a job or whatever, a banana skin on the pavement outside, when all that's taken away, what we are left with is our 'being'. I still have myself, my dignity, my capacity to relate to other people, and perhaps to encourage them. I found it a very, very powerful encounter.[4]

As the word itself implies, gr-atitude is an essential part of attitude. To acknowledge everything we have received, no matter how small the gift, is to ensure that we never take life for granted. That remarkable blind woman, Helen Keller, speaks eloquently of the art of gratitude:

---

[4] From a talk by Caroline Jones entitled 'Education of the Heart – the Compassionate Heart', given at the 1998 AHISA Pastoral Care Conference at St Joseph's College, Hunters Hill, Sydney.

> Most of us take life for granted … Only the deaf appreciate hearing; only the blind realize the manifold blessings that lie in sight … It is the same old story of not being grateful for what we have until we lose it; of not being conscious of health until we are ill … I, who am blind, can give one hint to those who see: use your eyes as if tomorrow you would be stricken blind. And the same method can be applied to the other senses. Hear the music of voices, the song of the bird, the mighty strains of an orchestra, as if you would be stricken deaf tomorrow. Touch each object you want to touch as if tomorrow your tactile sense would fail. Smell the perfume of flowers, taste with relish each morsel, as if tomorrow you could never smell and taste again. Make the most of every sense; glory in all the facets of pleasure and beauty which the world reveals to us.[5]

There was a wise old preacher who commented at one time that 'attitude determines altitude'. In other words, it is our attitude to life which determines how far, how long, how deep, how high we will progress. Prolific author and public speaker Stephen Covey makes a similar point when he refers to leadership 'from the inside out'. Proactive people subordinate feelings to values. Where reactive people absolve themselves of responsibility, the proactive person acknowledges that change must come from the inside out. 'If I really want to improve my situation, I can work on the one thing over which I have control – myself.'[6]

The true leader, therefore, begins from the inside out – with that capacity for vision, for self-reflection, for discernment between what is reactive and proactive in him or her, between the negative and the positive. The words of Robert M. Pirsig echo this same theme: 'The place to improve the world is first in one's own heart and head and hands – and then work outward from there.'[7]

---

[5] Helen Keller, 'Three Days to See', *The Atlantic*, January 1933.
[6] Stephen Covey, *The Seven Habits of Highly Effective People: Restoring the Character Ethic*, Information Australia, Melbourne, 1990, p. 90.
[7] *Zen and the Art of Motorcycle Maintenance*, William Morrow, 1974.

Reflections

Attitude and being proactive

I walked with my friend, a Quaker, to the newsstand the other night, and he bought a paper, thanking the newsie politely. The newsie didn't even acknowledge it. 'A sullen fellow, isn't he?' I commented. 'Oh, he's that way every night', shrugged my friend. 'Then why do you continue to be so polite to him?' I asked. 'Why not?' answered my friend. 'Why should I let him decide how I'm going to act?'

As I thought about this incident later, it occurred to me that the important word was 'act'. My friend acts toward people; most of us *react* toward them.

He has a sense of inner balance which is lacking in most of us; he knows who he is, what he stands for, how he should behave. He refused to return incivility for incivility, because then he would no longer be in command of his own conduct.

When we are enjoined in the Bible to return good for evil, we look upon this as a moral injunction – which it is. But it is also a psychological prescription for our emotional health.

Nobody is unhappier than the perpetual reactor. His centre of emotional gravity is not rooted within himself, where it belongs, but in the world outside him. His spiritual temperature is always being raised or lowered by the social climate around him, and he is a mere creature at the mercy of these elements.

Praise gives him a feeling of euphoria, which is false, because it does not last and it does not come from self-approval. Criticism depresses him more than it should, because it confirms his own secretly shaky opinion of himself. Snubs hurt him, and the merest suspicion of unpopularity in any quarter rouses him to bitterness.

A serenity of spirit cannot be achieved until we become the masters of our own actions and attitudes. To let another determine whether we shall be rude or gracious, elated or depressed, is to relinquish control over our own personalities, which is ultimately all we possess. The only true possession is self-possession.

Sydney J. Harris, *Reader's Digest*, July 1960

A Smile

A smile costs nothing
But gives much.
It enriches those who receive,
Without making poorer those who give.
It takes but a moment,
But the memory of it
Sometimes lasts forever.
None is so rich or mighty that
He can get along without it,
And none is so poor but that
He cannot be made rich by it.
A smile creates happiness in
The home, fosters good will in
Business, and is the countersign
Of friendship. It brings rest to
The weary, cheer to the
Discouraged, sunshine to the sad,
And it is nature's best
Antidote for trouble.
Yet it cannot be bought, begged,
Borrowed or stolen, for it is
Something that is of no value

To anyone until it is given away.
Some people are too tired to give
You a smile. Give them one of
Yours, as none needs a smile
So much as someone
Who has no more to give.

Source unknown

'God loves a cheerful giver.'
2 Corinthians 9:7

Attitude and seeing

Sr Deirdre Rofe IBVM, a good friend of mine and a friend to so many, died in Melbourne in August 2002, after a long illness. The following excerpt is from my 'Viewpoint' column, 23 August 2002.

I can remember Deirdre giving a splendid talk at the 1998 Jesuit Lenten Seminar Series on 'Education and Social Conscience'. She quoted the nineteenth century American philosopher, Jonathan Edwards: 'Saints do not see things others do not see. On the contrary. They see just what everyone else sees – but they see it differently.' Thank you, Deirdre, for helping us to see the world differently, always with that infectious laughter of yours. *Au revoir.*

Attitude and riches

You are richer than you were yesterday if you have laughed often, given something, forgiven even more, made a new friend, or made stepping stones of stumbling blocks; if you have thought more in terms of 'thyself' instead of 'myself'.

You are richer tonight than you were this morning if you have taken time to trace the handiwork of God in the commonplace things in life.

You are richer if a little child has smiled at you and a stray dog licked your hand, or if you looked for the best in others, and have given others the very best in you.

Russ Tyson, ABC broadcaster

Attitude and gr-atitude

We thank you, Lord, for the things of this world, in which
    we learn all we know and all we love of you.
We thank you for light and for darkness, for hopes and fears,
    for joy and sadness.
We thank you for the candles, which you give us to keep alight,
    for the air we breathe, and for the light we shed and share.
We thank you for the times and the seasons in which we know
    the ways of your presence to us, and the ache of our absence
    from you.
We thank you for that restlessness in which we seek you,
    and for the joy in which we find you.
We thank you that our friends are more than we can understand,
    and that they are not more than we can love.
We thank you for desert and oasis, for sea and shore,
    for hearth and horizon, for dreams and for tasks.
We thank you for coming to us; we thank you that you have
    gathered us this day to thank you.
We thank you for our own lives, and for those of all men and
    women.

Reflection from a St Ignatius' College staff Eucharist

Attitude and time

If I had my child to raise all over again,
I'd finger paint more and point the finger less.

I'd do less correcting and more connecting.
I'd take my eyes off my watch and watch more with my eyes.
I would care to know less and know to care more.
I'd take more hikes and fly more kites.
I'd stop playing serious and seriously play.
I'd run through more fields and gaze at the stars.
I'd do more hugging and less tugging.
I'd be firm less often and affirm much more.
I'd build self-esteem first and the house later.
I'd teach less about the love of power and more about the power of love.
Anonymous

I slept and dreamed that life was happiness,
Then I awoke and found out that life was service.
I served and I found out that in service happiness is found.
Rabindranath Tagore

Commonsense Be-attitudes

The Beatitudes are the Gospel's commentary on 'attitude'.

Blessed are those who can laugh at themselves; they will always have entertainment.

Blessed are those who can distinguish between a mountain and a molehill; they will save themselves a lot of trouble.

Blessed are those who can rest and sleep without looking for excuses; they will become wise.

Blessed are those who are intelligent enough not to take themselves too seriously; they will be appreciated.

Blessed are you if you can look seriously at small things and peacefully at serious things; you will go far in life.

Blessed are you if you can admire a smile and forget a scowl; your path will be sunlit.

Blessed are you if you can always interpret the attitudes of others with good will, even when appearances are to the contrary; you may seem naive, but that is the price of charity.

Blessed are those who think before acting and who laugh before thinking; they will avoid foolish mistakes.

Blessed are you if you know how to be silent and smile, even when you are interrupted, contradicted or walked on; the gospel is beginning to take root in your heart.

Blessed are you especially if you know how to recognize the Lord in all those you meet; you have found the true light, true wisdom.

Fr Joseph Folliet, *Petites béatitudes*

Attitude and gr-atitude again

If you woke up this morning with more health than illness ... you are more blessed than the million who will not survive this week.

If you have never experienced the danger of battle, the loneliness of imprisonment, the agony of torture, or the pangs of starvation ... you are ahead of 500 million people in the world.

If you can attend a church meeting without fear or harassment, arrest, torture, or death ... you are more blessed than three billion people in the world.

If you have food in the refrigerator, clothes on your back, a roof overhead and a place to sleep ... you are richer than 75 per cent of people in this world.

If you have money in the bank, in your wallet, and spare change in a dish someplace ... you are among the top eight per cent of the world's wealthy.

If you hold up your head with a smile on your face and are truly thankful ... you are lucky because the majority can, but most do not.

If you can hold someone's hand, hug them or even touch them on the shoulder ... you are blessed because you can offer a healing touch.

If you can read this message, someone was thinking of you, and, furthermore, you are better off than more than two billion people in the world who cannot read at all.

Have a good day, count your blessings, and pass this along to remind everyone else how lucky we all are.

Anonymous

Attitude and generosity

In the first reading tonight we heard a good deal about Time. Time is, after all, one of the most important gifts we can give to other people. The question to ask is what sort of time? Cheerful time? Generous time? Or do we give our time with a grudge and a complaint?

I read the other day of the little African boy who brought a special Christmas gift to his teacher. It was a superb sea-shell. The teacher was absolutely delighted with the beauty of the shell and asked the little boy where he found it. He said such shells could only be found at one particular beach many miles away from the school.

When the teacher responded with the words, 'Oh, you shouldn't have gone so far for a gift for me', the little boy said simply, 'The long walk was part of the gift.'

Homily, 16 August 2001

Attitude and humility

'Walk humbly with your God'
Micah 6:8

Paul Cézanne ranks among the world's greatest artists. Yet he painted for 35 years before receiving any recognition. When an art dealer finally discovered him and exhibited his paintings in Paris, Cézanne was overwhelmed. Entering the exhibition with his son, he could not believe what he saw. 'Look!' he said to his son, 'I can't believe it! They've even framed my paintings!'

The humility of Cézanne and the words of the prophet Micah invite me to reflect on humility. Who is one truly humble person I know? What makes true humility attractive?

> The true way to humility is not to stoop
> Until you are smaller than yourself,
> But to stand at your real height
> Against some higher nature
> That will show you
> What the real smallness
> Of your greatness is.

Phillips Brooks

Attitude and – life goes on!

Life is a sort of splendid torch which I have got hold of for the moment and I want to make it burn as brightly as possible before handing it over to future generations.

George Bernard Shaw

> I have learned that, no matter what happens, how bad it seems today, life goes on, and it will be better tomorrow.
> I've learned that you can tell a lot about a person by the way he or she handles three things – a rainy day, lost luggage, and tangled Christmas lights.
> I've learned that, regardless of your relationship with your parents, you will miss them when they are gone from your life.
> I've learned that making a living is not the same as making a life.
> I've learned that life sometimes gives you a second chance.

I've learned that you shouldn't go through life with a catcher's mitt on both hands. You need to be able to throw some things back.

I've learned that if you pursue happiness, it will elude you. But, if you focus on your family, your friends, and the needs of others, your work and doing the very best you can, happiness will find you.

I've learned that whenever I decide something with an open heart, I usually make the right decision.

I've learned that every day you should reach out and touch someone. People love those human touches – holding hands, a warm hug, or just a friendly pat on the back.

I've learned that I still have a lot to learn.

I've learned that you should pass this on to everyone that you care about.

I just did.

Sometimes they just need a little something to make them smile.

People will forget what you said; people will forget what you did;

But people never will forget how you made them feel.

adapted from Maya Angelou

Attitude and the present

When you cannot have what you think you would enjoy, you must learn to enjoy what you have or you will wish your life away while roses die at your feet.

Joan Chittister, *Songs of Joy*, p. 108.

Attitude acknowledged

From his very first day, our son thrived at Riverview. I truly believe that he epitomizes all the wonderful attributes of the Ignatian spirit. He lives life to the full, taking advantage of all opportunities given to him and repaying them a hundredfold! As parents we could not be more proud of him or more grateful for the huge part that Riverview played in his development. It is always a partnership between family and school, and for our son it was a winning combination!

When people ask me about Riverview I struggle to find the words to describe something almost intangible that happens for many young boys when they become part of the Riverview family. I think foremost it is a sense of pride in their school, a privilege to belong, but one that carries responsibilities.

His teachers, coaches, tutors and housemaster, challenged him to 'have a go'. Our son was encouraged to believe in himself, and was recognized and applauded for his individual gifts. He was never going to be a 'star' athlete, actor, musician or academic, but as a person he was admired for his loyalty, determination, application and commitment.

Despite a lifetime struggle with his learning difficulty, our son's determination and commitment with his studies resulted in a wonderful HSC result and after a student exchange overseas he will commence a Business degree at UTS. What an enormous achievement for a young man whom many thought would never be able to read!

From a parent's letter of gratitude for the school

Attitude and youth

Youth is not a time of life; it is a state of mind. It is the freshness of the deeper springs of life.

Nobody grows old merely by living a number of years. People grow old by deserting their ideals. Whether 60 or 16, every human being may experience wonder, the undaunted challenge of events, the unfailing, childlike appetite for the future, the joy in living. For you are as young as your faith, as old as your doubt; as young as your self-confidence, as old as your despair.

As long as your heart receives messages of beauty hope, cheer, courage, and power from God and from your fellow human beings, you are young.

Attitude and gr-atitude again!

Dear God, in most of our prayers we ask or pray for something or someone, such as the bushfire victims or the sick. Today, however, I would like to thank you for what you have given us. We have our health, our families, people who care for us, our sight, good minds and are physically well. So many people we have seen do not have these things and are not nearly as gifted as ourselves.

I would like to thank you for the opportunities that we have, and that many others dream of. I would like to thank you for the people who are so prepared to give up their time for the less well off, such as the nurses, teachers and missionaries of this world. Thank you for the goodness this world is capable of. In thanking you we say, 'Our Father, who art in heaven …'

Year 11 student prayer

Attitude and suffering

A sympathetic friend leaned close to a disabled woman and whispered, 'Affliction does so colour life, doesn't it?'

'Yes', the handicapped woman replied, 'but thank God I can choose the colour.'

We may not always be able to escape the raw realities of life as they confront us but with God's help we can shape them. Faith doesn't immunize us from difficulty. But it does radically alter our attitude towards our difficulties.

Living as people of soul

*You are a second world in miniature,
the sun and moon are within you,
and also the stars.*

Origen

Towards the end of July 1999, one of my best Jesuit friends and my religious community Superior at the time, John Xavier Ramsay, died of coronary heart failure. If the truth be known, he should have died 13 years earlier in Melbourne, but skilful heart bypass surgery gave him the opportunity to continue being a powerful influence for good on many people in two school communities. Large of heart and physical stature, yet somewhat retiring in demeanor, 'Rams', as he was affectionately known, was an intensely passionate man. Rowing, military history and pageantry, his family, his students, the Society of Jesus, were the loves of his life. And he loved them with a passion.

Following his coronary occlusion on 29 July and the irreparable brain damage he suffered as a consequence, there was a 24-hour period of waiting for death without life-support systems. Room 1 at Royal North Shore Private Hospital became something of a place of pilgrimage as students and friends came to say their farewells or simply offer support to the family.

I will never forget one scene late on the afternoon of the day that John died. After school finished, a very shy and gauche young Riverview oarsman came to the hospital and asked me if I would accompany him to visit Father Ramsay. After preparing him for the bedroom scene, I took him inside and he immediately produced a letter which he asked me to read. There we were, the three of us – dear John Ramsay comatose in his bed, breathing heavily and arhythmically, the young rower crying unashamedly, and I myself equally tearful – as I read out this letter of thanks to 'Rams' for everything he had done for this young man. It was a letter full of soul to a man of great soul.

At the beginning of 2002 in Australia we were confronted regularly in the media with many pictures of refugees and asylum-seekers in their hell-hole of a detention centre confinement at Woomera. Photos of children and adults on hunger strike, with their lips stapled together, made us ask: where has the heart of Australia disappeared if we are treating other human beings like this? In late July, Father Frank Brennan sj related one story of the Woomera situation in his homily for the Feast of St Ignatius:

> Let me tell you about just one woman at Woomera. She is a single mum. She is there with her seven-year-old son. With me on Monday was an Australian writer who had never been to Woomera before. As this woman told her story, she paused, looked at the writer, laughed nervously, and said, 'I'm sorry. You're very upset, aren't you?' Despite her suffering, she had time for the other person, attentive to his pain, careful about his needs. This woman said she had a choice in life: 'Freedom or death.' Suffering and isolation make our choices in life more stark. This woman knows that if she died, the government would have to foster her child into the freedom of the Australian community. In love and commitment to her son, she sees death for herself as an option, a way to freedom for her son.

Together with the distressing photos of the Woomera detention centre, Australians were also treated to heartening pictures of courageous firefighters risking their lives to save people and their homes from the bushfires that seem to have multiplied around the country in recent years. They were a strong reminder that Australia had not lost its compassionate heart altogether and that we still had some quality of soul as a nation.

On this theme of heart and soul, I like to return often to a quotation I have utilized many times over the years in different contexts. It remains valuable because it has stood the test of time. The author, Dr Edmond Barnola, a parent at a French Jesuit high school, was writing about parental expectations of that school, an all-boys school:

> I hope that we have not sent our sons here because their very being here confers a peculiar social distinction, or because we find it desirable that our sons should be educated among boys of their own social class ... We are not looking for a seminary for mundane animals. Nor do we want a pot-hunting academy which flaunts its examination successes like so many sporting trophies; a training camp for intellectual athletes. Nor again, if I may risk giving scandal, have we chosen this school because it provides good religious instruction ... It is for none of these reasons that we send our boys here. Our real care is for what I may describe as their quality of soul.[1]

'Soul', according to Thomas Moore, author of *Care of the Soul*, 'is tied to life in all its particulars – good food, satisfying conversation, genuine friends, and experiences that stay in the memory and touch the heart.' It is 'not a thing, but a quality or a dimension of experiencing life and ourselves. It has to do with depth, value, relatedness, heart, and personal substance.'[2] For psychologist James Hillman, soul is 'a perspective rather than a substance, a viewpoint toward things rather than a thing itself.'[3]

---

[1] Edmond Barnola, 'What we expect of a school: A parent's view', *Jesuit Secondary Education*, 1975, no. 4, March 1976, pp. 26-28.
[2] Thomas Moore, *Care of the Soul: A Guide for Cultivating Depth and Sacredness in Everyday Life*, HarperCollins, New York, pp. xi, 5.
[3] James Hillman, *Re-Visioning Psychology*, HarperCollins, New York, 1992, p. xvi.

'Soul' and 'heart' are obviously very closely related. *The Catholic Catechism* defines 'heart' very helpfully in this way:

> The heart is the dwelling-place where I am, where I live; according to the Semitic or biblical expression, the heart is the place 'to which I withdraw'. The heart is our hidden centre, beyond the grasp of our reason and of others; only the Spirit of God can fathom the human heart and know it fully. The heart is the place of decision, deeper than our psychic drives. It is the place of truth, where we choose life or death. It is the place of encounter, because as images of God we live in relation: it is the place of covenant (para 2563).

One of the compliments I cherish most came from a parent whose last son was finishing at the school. She wrote to me: 'I may not remember all you said, but I know how you made me feel – valued.' For some reason it reminded me of that marvellous passage from the novel *Zorba the Greek* where Zorba is saying, 'One day when I was a child, an old man took me on his knee and placed his hand on my head as if he were giving me a blessing. "Alexis", he said, "I'm going to tell you a secret. You are too small to understand now, but you will understand when you are bigger. Listen, little one. Neither the seven stories of Heaven nor the seven stories of earth are enough to contain God, but a person's heart can contain God. So, be careful, Alexis – and my blessing be with you – never to wound another person's heart."'

In sharp contrast, the following true story took place on a British Airways flight from Johannesburg to London. A middle-aged, well-off white woman had found herself sitting next to a black man. She called the cabin crew attendant over to complain about her seating.

> 'What seems to be the problem, Madam?' asked the attendant.
> 'Can't you see?' she said. 'You've sat me next to a Kaffir. I can't possibly sit next to this disgusting human. Find me another seat!'

'Please calm down, Madam', the stewardess replied. 'The flight is very full today, but I'll tell you what I'll do. I'll go and check and see if we have any seats available in business or first class.'

The woman cocked a snooty look at the outraged black man beside her (not to mention many of the surrounding passengers). A few minutes later the stewardess returned with the good news, which she delivered to the lady, who could not help but look at the people around her with a smug and self-satisfied grin.

'Madam, unfortunately, as I suspected, economy is full. I've spoken to the cabin services director and business class is also full. However, we do have one seat in first class.'

Before the woman had a chance to answer, the stewardess continued – 'It is most extraordinary to make this kind of upgrade, however, and I have had to get special permission from the Captain. But, given the circumstances, the Captain felt that it was outrageous that someone be forced to sit next to such an obnoxious person.'

With which the stewardess turned to the black man sitting next to the woman, and said: 'So if you would like to get your things, Sir, I have your seat ready for you …'

On hearing this exchange, apparently the surrounding passengers gave a loud ovation while the black man walked up to the front of the airplane.

And, of course, there is a moral to this story. It can be best summed up by the following saying :

> People may forget what you said,
> People may forget what you did,
> But people will never forget how you made them feel.

People with soul are going to be people of heart, people of hope, and people of courage. I can recall a lovely line spoken at the funeral, in November 2000, of Tony Rae, former Headmaster of Newington

College, by his daughter Jenny: 'My father and I might not always have seen eye to eye, but we always saw heart to heart.' All great loves, to use a sporting metaphor, are a marathon of the heart. Unlike 'falling in love', which is more of an emotional sprint, committed love requires constant training and discipline – patience, forgiveness, trust, hope, and endurance.

Recently I was given a little book of quotations from Morris West's writings, and I was struck by the following words from one of his novels: 'Falling in love – that's for children. But loving, that's like the best wine … to decant slowly and hold gently, and savour and sip. You don't grow a great vintage. You create it.'

Similarly, Ardis Whitman wrote that 'Love is not a single act, but a climate in which we live, a lifetime venture in which we are always learning, discovering, growing. It is not destroyed by a single failure, or won by a single caress. Love is a climate – a climate of the heart.'

People of soul are good at creating a climate of the heart. They are people of hope and frequently in the most difficult of circumstances. For a long time I have found inspiration in the challenging words of the young pharmacist, Walter Mikac, when he spoke at the funeral service for his wife and daughters slaughtered in the madness of the Port Arthur massacre in 1996: 'Do not take your partner for granted, do not take your children for granted, do not take life for granted. Most importantly, do not take tomorrow for granted. The power of love and creation will always triumph over the power of destruction and revenge.'

Cynicism and its first cousin negativism are usually a refuge for the faint-hearted. In this context I have enjoyed quoting often the story of a young boy and his grandfather leading a donkey down a road. Someone laughed at them for being stupid and not riding the donkey. So the grandfather rode the donkey until someone criticized him for making the boy walk. Then the boy rode the donkey until someone criticized him for lack of respect for elders. Finally both rode the donkey until someone criticized them for being cruel to animals.

Our world, and particularly the young people for whom we care, need constant injections of hope. Every community needs its incurable but realistic optimists. Indeed, we want our young people to catch the spirit of what Anglo-Irish playwright George Bernard Shaw once wrote:

> I am of the opinion that my life belongs to the community, and as long as I live, it is my privilege to do for it whatever I can. I want to be thoroughly used up when I die, for the harder I work, the more I live. Life is no 'brief candle' for me. It is a sort of splendid torch which I have got hold of for a moment, and I want to make it burn as brightly as possible before handing it on to future generations.[4]

People of soul also possess an indomitable courage. I remember being most moved by the picture of the young woman, Elaine Duch, emerging in a wheelchair from hospital after four months of medical treatment for the horrific burns to 77 per cent of her body suffered in the September 11 terrorist attack on the World Trade Center in 2001. The human spirit, our soul, can be so strong in the face of fearful adversity.

Similarly, the Dutch Jew Etty Hillesum, was able to rise above the hellish circumstances of a concentration camp in Auschwitz and write about her German captors in 1942:

> But above the one narrow path still left to us stretches the sky, intact. They can't do anything to us, they really can't. They can harass us, they can rob us of our material goods, of our freedom of movement, but we ourselves forfeit our greatest assets by our compliance. By our feelings of being persecuted, humiliated and oppressed. By our own hatred ... We may, of course, be sad and

---

[4] George Bernard Shaw, 'Art and Public Money', *Sussex Daily News*, 7 March, 1907.

depressed by what has been done to us; that is only human and understandable. However: our greatest injury is one we inflict upon ourselves. I find life beautiful and I feel free. The sky within me is as wide as the one stretching above my head. I believe in God and I believe in man and I say so without embarrassment. Life is hard, but that is no bad thing.[5]

To help our young people develop a strong quality of soul, we have to look carefully at the quality of our own companionship with them. Perhaps the most important ingredient in this venture is our own self-awareness. We have to be so alert to what is going on in ourselves, so alive to our own agenda, so capable of listening to ourselves before we can be of any real assistance to others. We must become accustomed to tuning into our moods and the simple process of self-reflection this evokes.

Out of what level is most of today being lived? Is it a whole host of surface and superficial things which is making me feel empty? Or is my day coming from a different source which brings me deep peace, the sort of consolation associated with the true self? Self-awareness, therefore, is vital to the quality of our companionship. If we are unable to hear what is going on in ourselves, we will so easily allow it to interfere with our listening to others.

To cultivate quality of soul in others, we need to have some time for our own souls. Professor Ron Heifetz of Harvard University speaks about the need for having a balcony in our lives if we are to understand the sometimes frenzied dance of events going on around us. Without such a balcony, we can easily be swept up in the dance of life and lose our perspective. Where is the balcony for my soul?

---

[5] Etty Hillesum, *An Interrupted Life: The Diaries of Etty Hillesum 1941-43*, Pantheon Books, New York, 1984, p. 151.

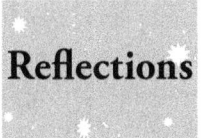

Reflections

Love is a marathon of the heart

Love is a temporary madness, it erupts like volcanoes and then subsides. And when it subsides you have to make a decision. You have to work out whether your roots have so entwined together that it is inconceivable that you should ever part. Because this is what love is. Love is not breathlessness, it is not excitement, it is not the promulgation of promises of eternal passion … That is just being 'in love', which any fool can do. Love itself is what is left over when being in love has burned away, and this is both an art and a fortunate accident. Your mother and I had it, we had roots that grew towards each other underground, and when all the pretty blossom had fallen from our branches we found that we were one tree and not two.

Louis de Bernières, *Captain Corelli's Mandolin*

Love and giving

Some years ago, divers located a 400-year-old ship off the coast of Northern Ireland. Among the treasures found on the sunken ship was a man's wedding ring. When it was cleaned up, the divers noticed that it had an inscription on it. Engraved on the wide band was a hand holding a heart. Under the engraving was the inscription: 'I have nothing more to give you'.

Love and vulnerability

'Lent is a time to listen to our lives' is the title of an article by Franciscan Father Richard Rohr in the *National Catholic Reporter* sent to me by a parent prior to the season of Lent. What follows are the first two paragraphs.

'The young man who cannot cry is a savage. The old man who cannot weep is a fool.' Native Aphorism

What got me into this work of creating liminal space and understanding initiation was my observation of the state of the male of the species, clergy and laymen. We are not in good shape. We do not tend to naturally understand spirituality. In fact, I am convinced the male is naturally resistant to spirituality's language of intimacy, surrender, patience and trust. Men like roles instead of process, dressing up instead of dressing down.

To paraphrase the Rogers and Hammerstein song, the male 'has to be taught, he has to be carefully taught.' And this is why almost all ancient cultures deemed male initiation necessary for the survival of the tribe. The male must be taught 'the tears of things' before you can dare invest him in power, or he will always abuse that power. Initiation is always an intentional journey into powerlessness, so the man will know how to use power well.

A light in the darkness – the Christian as lamplighter

At the Valete Mass [2002] I reminded the boys and their parents that in the time before there were electric lights on our city streets, a person would have the responsibility of being the lamplighter and lighting the gas lamps at dusk and extinguishing them before dawn. Going down one street and up another, he would have people watching him doing his work. They would watch him until the sun went down and could not see him any more. But they could see new light come forth.

This is for me a wonderful image of what a Christian life is all about and what lies behind this challenge for all of us. Those who are Christians continue to light new lights and we can follow their path by the lights they have left behind. They become for us a light in the darkness. A true Christian, therefore, is one whose track you can follow by the light he or she leaves burning.

In all the darkness of stories about Bali, the gunman at Monash

University, and the sniper in Washington, we need to remember that we are meant to be a light of hope in our world. The way we care for other people, the way we affirm and encourage them, is our way of being a lamplighter. Each time you light a candle, you might remember your role as a lamplighter and the beautiful prayer which is used in Salisbury Cathedral, England that reads:

> Lighting a candle is a prayer:
> When we have gone it stays alight
> kindling in the hearts and minds
> of others the prayers
> we have already offered for them
> and for others.
> For the sad, the sick, and the suffering
> and prayers of thankfulness too.
>
> Lighting a candle is a parable:
> Burning itself out,
> It gives light to others.
> Christ gave himself for others.
> He calls us to give ourselves.
>
> Lighting a candle is a symbol:
> Of love and hope,
> Of light and warmth.
> Our world needs them all.

'Viewpoint', 25 October 2002

A friendship blessing

May you be blessed with good friends.
May you learn to be a good friend to your self.
May you be able to journey to that place in your soul where there is great love, warmth, feeling and forgiveness.

> May this change you.
> May it transfigure that which is negative, distant or
> cold in you.
> May you be brought in to the real passion, kinship and
> affinity of belonging.
> May you treasure your friends.
> May you be good to them and may you be there for them;
> may they bring you all the blessings, challenges, truth
> and light that you need for your journey.
>
> May you never be isolated; but may you always be
> in the gentle nest of belonging with your *anam cara*.

John O'Donohue, *Anam Cara*, 1997, p. 60

Quality of soul

It doesn't interest me what you do for a living. I want to know what you ache for, and if you dare to dream of meeting your heart's longing.

It doesn't interest me how old you are. I want to know if you will risk looking like a fool for love, for your dream, for the adventure of being alive.

It doesn't interest me what planets are squaring your moon. I want to know if you have touched the centre of your own sorrow, if you have been opened by life's betrayals or have become shrivelled and closed from fear of further pain! I want to know if you can sit with pain, mine or your own, without moving to hide it or fix it.

I want to know if you can be with joy, mine or your own; if you can dance with wildness and let the ecstasy fill you to the tips of your fingers and toes without cautioning us to be careful, to be realistic, to remember the limitations of being human.

It doesn't interest me if the story you are telling me is true. I want to know if you can disappoint another to be true to yourself; if you can bear the accusation of betrayal and not betray your own soul; if you can be faithless and therefore trustworthy.

I want to know if you can see beauty even when it's not pretty, every day, and if you can source your own life from its presence.

I want to know if you can live with failure, yours and mine, and still stand on the edge of the lake and shout to the silver of the full moon, 'Yes!'

It doesn't interest me to know where you live or how much money you have. I want to know if you can get up after the night of grief and despair, weary and bruised to the bone, and do what needs to be done to feed the children.

It doesn't interest me who you know or how you came to be here. I want to know if you will stand in the centre of the fire with me and not shrink back.

It doesn't interest me where or what or with whom you have studied. I want to know what sustains you, from the inside, when all else falls away.

I want to know if you can be alone with yourself and if you truly like the company you keep in the empty moments.

'The Invitation' by Oriah Mountain Dreamer, from *Dreams of Desire*, Oriah House, 1995

Living with heart

Tuesdays with Morrie by Mitch Albom (Hodder Headline, pp. 33-34) is the lovely story of a young man visiting each Tuesday his old university professor who is dying.

The eighties happened. The nineties happened. Death and sickness and getting fat and going bald happened. I traded lots of dreams for a bigger paycheck, and I never realized I was doing it.

Yet here was Morrie talking with the wonder of our College years, as if I'd simply been on a long vacation.

'Have you found someone to share your heart with?' he asked.

'Are you giving to your community?

'Are you at peace with yourself?

'Are you as human as you can be?'

Soul and compassion

… I am so pleased to be able to tell you that I now know that he has become the young man that I had hoped he would become on sending him, all those years ago, to Riverview. He is a fine sensitive person with a strong sense of the Ignatian spirit, a love of God in himself and others and above all he has the imagination to be able to place himself in the position of others – I believe that without this one is not able to be truly compassionate or to be able to imagine a better world.

He will be well equipped to take his part in building a better world – not just a shallow and fanciful place but one informed by so much more. I thank you all from the bottom of my heart.

An excerpt from a Year 12 mother's letter following her son's graduation.

Friendship

Think where man's glory most begins and ends,
and say my glory was I had such friends.
W. B. Yeats, 'The Municipal Galley Revisited'

The optimist's creed

Promise yourself –

To be so strong that nothing can disturb your peace of mind

To talk health, happiness and prosperity to every person you meet.

To make all your friends feel that there is something in them.

To look at the sunny side of everything and make your optimism come true.

To think only of the best, to work only for the best, and to expect only the best.

To be just as enthusiastic about the success of others as you are about your own.

To forget the mistakes of the past and press on to the greater
achievements of the future.
To wear a cheerful countenance at all times and give
every creature you meet a smile.
To give so much time to improvement of yourself that
you have not time to criticize others.
To be too large for worry, too noble for anger, too strong
for fear, and too happy to permit the presence of trouble.
Christian D. Larson

Soul and surprise

I asked for strength,
that I might achieve greatness.
I was made weak
that I might learn humbly to obey.
I asked for health,
that I might do greater things,
I was given infirmity,
that I might do better things.
I asked for riches,
that I might be happy,
I was given poverty,
that I might be wise.
I asked for power,
that I might have the praise of men,
I was given weakness,
that I might feel the need of God.
I asked for all things,
that I might enjoy life.
I was given life,
that I might enjoy all things.

I got nothing that I asked for –
But everything I hoped for.
Almost despite myself,
My unspoken prayers were answered.
I am, among all men,
Most richly blessed.

from A Christian Confederate soldier's prayer

Soul and risk

To laugh is to risk appearing a fool.
To weep is to risk appearing sentimental.
To reach out for another person is to risk involvement.
To expose your feelings is to risk being your true self.
To place your dreams and ideas before the crowd is to risk their rejection.
To love is to risk not being loved in return.
To live is to risk dying.
To hope is to risk despair.
To try is to risk failure.
But risks must be taken, because the greatest hazard in life is to risk nothing.
The person who risks nothing, does nothing, has nothing, is nothing.
This person may avoid suffering and sorrow, but cannot learn, feel, change, grow, love, or live.
This person is chained by their certitude, a slave who has forfeited all freedom.
Only a person who risks is free.
The pessiminst complains about the wind
The optimist wxpects it to change
and the realist adjusts the sails.

William Arthur Ward

Soul and teaching

Only the brave should teach. The men and women whose integrity cannot be shaken, whose minds are enlightened enough to understand the high calling of the teacher, whose hearts are unshakably loyal to the young, whatever the interests of those who are in power.

There is no hope for our world unless we can educate a different kind of man and woman. I put the teacher higher than any other person today in world society, in responsibility and in opportunity. Only those who love the young should teach. Teaching's not a way to make a livelihood; the livelihood is incidental. Teaching is a vocation. It is as sacred as priesthood, as innate as a desire, as inseparable as the genius which compels a great artist.

If a teacher has not the concern of humanity, the love for living creatures, the vision of the priest and of the artist, that person must not teach. Teachers who hate to teach can only have pupils who hate to learn. Great and true teachers think of the child, dream of the child, see visions not of themselves but in the flowering of the child into adulthood. They think of the child first and always not of themselves.

It takes courage to be a teacher and it takes unalterable love for the child; only the brave should teach.

Pearl S. Buck

Jesus the teacher

He never taught in a classroom.
He had no tools to work with, no blackboards, maps or charts.
He used no subject outlines, kept no records, gave no grades,
 and his only text was ancient and well-worn.
His students were the poor, the lame, the deaf, the blind, the
 outcast –
and his method was the same with all who came to hear and
 learn.

He opened eyes with faith; he opened ears with simple truth;
and opened hearts with love, a love born of forgiveness.
A gentle man, a humble man, he asked and won no honours,
no gold awards of tribute to his expertise or wisdom.
And yet this quiet teacher from the hills of Galilee has fed the needs,
fulfilled the hopes, and changed the lives of many millions.
For what he taught brought heaven to earth
and God's heart to all people.

Soul and compassion

'The spirit cannot die', wrote Czech poet Franz Mark, 'in no circumstances, under no torment, despite whatever calumnies, in no bleak places.' The concentration camps indeed proved that. The following prayer was found scribbled on a piece of wrapping-paper near the body of a dead child at Ravensbrück camp where 92,000 women and children died.

'O Lord, remember not only the men and women of good will, but also those of ill-will. But do not remember all the suffering they have inflicted on us; remember the fruits we have bought, thanks to this suffering – our comradeship, our loyalty, our humility, our courage, our generosity, the greatness of heart which has grown out of all this, and when they come to the judgment let all the fruits that we have borne be their forgiveness.'

Only one who had plumbed the depths of suffering could have learned so much compassion.

Mary Craig, 'Take Up Your Cross', *The Way*, 13, 1973, pp. 22-32

Soul and music

In July, 1992, there appeared in *The New York Times Magazine* a photo of a musician named Vedran Smailóvic. He was a cellist in the war-torn country of Bosnia, and every day he used to come to the centre of the town and play his cello. It was a time of violent civil war in the city, with everyone becoming an enemy of someone else. Except for this one man, who came to the street corner every day to play his cello.

There he was in the photo – middle-aged, longish hair, great bushy moustache, dressed in formal evening clothes – sitting in a fire-charred chair in the middle of a street, where mortar fire had struck a breadline just the previous day killing 22 people. A member of the Sarajevo Opera Orchestra, he was doing what he loved and knew best – he was playing his cello. He thought there was little he could do about hate or war as a musician. So every day for 22 days, knowing he might be shot or beaten, he braved sniper and artillery fire to play the most beautiful music he knew – Albinoni's *Adagio in G Minor* – a piece of music constructed from a manuscript fragment found in the ruins of the fire-bombed city of Dresden after World War II.

To me this photo of the cellist is a picture of great hope, of God's goodness. His music was stronger than hate, his courage stronger than fear. In time other musicians came to join him in the street and play their music, Their courage was contagious and eventually the fighting stopped.

Homily, Perth, 19 October 2000

'Living in an unfair world, life isn't fair'

I doubt if anyone would disagree. We create a fantasy of the way we'd like life to be but rarely does day-to-day reality come anywhere near our ideal picture. As a result, we experience a wide range of emotions – anger, frustrations, bitterness, disappointment, fear, sadness – that take away our ability to enjoy life.

An office poster reads: 'One day I shall burst my buds of calm and blossom fully into hysteria.'

Or, a saleswoman cheerfully said to a customer, 'Have a nice day!' and the lady responded, 'I have other plans.'

Or, how about Charlie Brown who said, 'I have a new philosophy. I'm only going to dread one day at a time.'

What is the key to living in a world of unfairness?

It is to admit and accept that often life can be unfair. And it's important to find the hand of God not solely in the precision and goodness of life but also in the courage, determination and resilience of the human spirit.

It is to find the hand of God in the willingness and ability of you and me to go on living and living fully even when we find out how unfair the world can be.

Expecting the world to treat you fairly because you're a Christian is like expecting the bull not to attack you because you are a vegetarian.

Harold Kushner in *Why do bad things happen to good people?* puts it this way: '"Why does it happen?" is a futile question that focuses on the past. The real question is now that it has happened, what are we going to do about it? How will you respond in a way that goes on affirming life?'

We need to realize and accept that life isn't the way it is supposed to be. Life is simply the way it is. How we choose to respond to life's challenges determines our experience of life. Ralph Waldo Emerson wrote, 'What lies behind us and what lies before us are tiny matters compared to what lies within us.'

What is the key to living in a world of unfairness?

We've all witnessed a solitary blade of grass staking its claim in the crack of a concrete sidewalk or a tree growing defiantly out of the side of a granite cliff. How can the tree survive in such an environment?

How can we survive and keep growing in an unfair world when the odds seem stacked against us? Where do we find nourishment and strength when the well runs dry? The realities of life have a way of destroying our optimism. However, there is still room for hope.

The difference between optimism and hope is that optimism depends on human ability; hope has God as its foundation.

'Nothing can separate us from the love of God in Christ.'

Hope isn't the certainty that the world is going to be fair and that life will work out exactly as planned. Hope says that even when bad things do happen to good people, you'll still be okay.

Hope is what we find at the bottom of our well. Hope, given to us as a gift from God, is the one thing we can depend on when everything else crumbles.

Hope is what gets us through, even when we thought we wouldn't get through.

Hope allows us to put one foot in front of the other as we hear God's whisper, 'Keep going. I'm right behind you.'

> Rev Steven H. Koski, Minister, Brougham Place Uniting Church, Director, The Cairnmillar Institute.

The heart

Waiting for the truth to unfold is not easy in a world that expects quick results, easy answers. That is a form of hope that demands great courage as well as great patience and the ability to believe that in the end there will be no winners and losers, only the truth.

> It is the heart that gives, the fingers just let go.
> Nigerian proverb

Living with success and failure

And he sees the vision splendid of the sunlit plains extended,
And at night the wondrous glory of the everlasting stars.

Banjo Patterson

One of the low points for parents and teachers trying to help young people to develop a balanced attitude to success and failure was surely the slogan in vogue during the Atlanta Olympic Games: 'Silver medals are for losers!'

Such a 'win at all costs' attitude is addictive and is alien to those parents and teachers who have the best interests of their children at heart. 'Success is not a gospel value', a wise Jesuit spiritual director once reminded me. We should be constantly at pains to help young people see that winning and losing are just different points in a long process of preparation, team discipline, perseverance, and sportsmanship. Success lies in the quality of one's striving and not necessarily in the capturing of any trophies. Sadly, our 'winners are grinners' culture would want us to see it differently.

On a slightly different tack, I can remember the great Australian Rugby Captain, Nick Farr-Jones, commenting once that when he first began playing with the Wallabies, they did not win many matches. The reason, he said, was that the team 'focused on the scoreboard and not on the process'. In other words, they were preoccupied with their and their opponents' score lines, and had lost sight of all the ingredients of their play that might achieve and even improve on those scores. Those people with a 'bottom line' or scoreboard mentality will always have a narrow and distorted view of success. Ironically, in neglecting the process they will also be deprived of much success too.

School communities are constantly walking a tightrope in this difficult area of success. Harking back to what historian Greg Dening in our Introduction terms a 'never-to-be-resolved contradiction', schools need to ensure they are successful in giving their students well-honed professional and technical skills for their future careers. This is the success which many students and parents expect. On the other hand, what our students need – and deserve – includes, but transcends, this 'worldly' success based on marketable skills. The real measure of success in our schools lies in who our students become.

During the many years I have sat on stage for speech days and prize-giving ceremonies, I have always experienced mixed emotions. In listening to all the glowing accolades showered on some students for their fine achievements, I know that there is an equal number of students sitting in the audience who will not be acknowledged. Their success might not have been in the academic or co-curricular sphere, but their innate goodness as people of positive influence in the school community stamps them as successful by any reckoning. Yet they are not publicly recognised or acclaimed for this. Dr Simon Longstaff, the Chief Executive Officer for the St James Ethics Centre, captured this well when he wrote:

> Some think that heroes are
> forged in the white heat of the
> dangerous moment.
> But there is another kind of hero,

> the person of quiet decency whose achievement
> is built over an entire career.
> We are held by the intensity of lightning,
> yet to fail to mention the thunder that rolls on
> into the distance long after the lightning's
> moment has passed.
> We are captured by the tumultuous descent
> of the waterfall while the steady progress of
> the river is ignored.
> And we marvel at the ocean's power,
> unaware of the fact that we stand upon
> ground claimed for us by the silent witness
> of the ancient cliff.

In the words of Jonathan Sacks, when speaking about the late Cardinal Basil Hume, 'heroes are those who turn strangers into friends.' True heroes, therefore, gain success where it matters most in life – in being a friend to others and in being people of 'quiet decency'.

During my last year as Rector of Riverview, patently one of the most successful years in the College's history in terms of co-curricular supremacy, there were many opportunities to reflect on the true meaning of 'success'. At one school assembly, I proposed that, if success were measured by making friends and creating a climate of happiness around us, then one of the school's neighbours, Matthew Shield, was the most successful person in the Association of the Great Public Schools.

Slightly intellectually impaired, though very sensitive and careful not to intrude on others' space, Matthew has the wonderful gift of remembering and affirming all manner of people across all schools in the Association. He creates laughter and happiness around him wherever he goes, and the Riverview students have adopted him, for well over a decade now, as their number one supporter. He travels with them in the bus to away games, attends by invitation their end of season celebrations, and occasionally offers brief and well chosen words of wisdom at school assemblies. All sorts of school dignitaries, like visiting principals and school council chairs, warm to him and accept his gentle chiding that their school will have no chance at all against Riverview in the upcoming sporting fixture. Indeed, I can remember seeing him sitting in the front row of an opposing school's basketball team as they prepared to have their premiership photo taken.

'Mattie' might have elevated one-eyed barracking to an art form, but his capacity to affirm people and celebrate life makes him extremely successful by any criterion. He is living evidence that success is something inside us and flows from the inside out. It is about having an impact on the lives of other people. If success is to be defined in terms of leaving a 'thumbprint' on the people around us, then Mattie Shield must be one of the most successful people in the GPS. Success, therefore, is something on the inside; it's about the sort of person we are.

Ultimately, of course, the success of any school can only be judged by the graduates it produces, and that judgment can only be made some 15 years or so after they have left school. What sort of person have they become? Have they nurtured those qualities of soul planted in them at home and at school? Are they beginning to leave a thumbprint on their world such that it is a better place for their presence? Time will tell the true story.

Rabindranath Tagore once wrote: 'The mountain remains unmoved at seeming defeat by the mist.' In other words, failure is not necessarily failure at all. It may simply be part of the process of becoming what we are really meant to be. Until we know defeat, we are almost never capable of real success. Sir Winston Churchill once said, 'Success is the ability to go from one failure to another with no loss of enthusiasm.'

St Ignatius invited us 'to work as if success depends on ourselves alone, but with the heartfelt conviction that we are doing nothing and God everything.' On a different tack, that great religious icon of India,

Mother Teresa, was once asked why she continued to work in the appalling conditions of Calcutta when she had not succeeded in changing them very much. Her profound answer was that it was much more important to be faithful than to be successful.

In our schools we are constantly asking our young people to strive for success, but are we doing enough to help them to cope with failure, very often perceived failure? It is worth remembering that 'we are who we are as much because of our gaps and failures as because of our strengths'.[1]

Care of the soul means respecting all its emotions and fantasies, and failure provides us with the opportunity to savour those feelings of limitation which are part and parcel of life. The narcissist indulges in failure – 'I'm a failure. I can't do anything right.' What we want, however, is to observe how failure affects the heart, so that those feelings might re-connect us with success.

It is true that the soul is most powerfully affected when we feel inferior, hurt, defenceless, vulnerable, when we experience failure. Indeed, it is a strange fact that 'soul appears most easily in those places where we feel most inferior.'[2] All of us know that choosing to love will open spaces of immense beauty and joy, but we will also be hurt.

Love requires vulnerability, it demands defencelessness. As Patrick O'Sullivan argues, 'When vulnerability meets power, the result is alienation; but when vulnerability is met by vulnerability, the result is intimacy. The only way into intimacy is through vulnerability.'[3] As carers of the soul, we honour the symptoms of hurt and defencelessness, inferiority and failure in those we serve, rather than leap to the bottom line and try to solve some imaginary problem they might have. We must observe

---

[1] Thomas Moore, *Care of the Soul*, p. 51.
[2] ibid.
[3] Patrick O'Sullivan SJ, *Sure Beats Selling Cardigans: Fostering Our Relationship with God*, David Lovell Publishing, 1995, p. 8.

and follow both the song lines and the pain lines. The only way out of hurt is through it.

This is not the prevailing message in our society, however. Too often we are taught that 'suffering can be avoided or anaesthetized with drugs, alcohol, sex, exciting experiences, "raging" … that money solves problems and buys happiness; that conscience is negotiable; that life is something we can create and terminate at convenience.'[4] Such is the proclaimed wisdom of the all-popular 'soapie' on television, which relishes the glamorous, busy edge of things but is 'nervous of the interior, the desert, silence. It is unfashionable to express concepts of surrender or humility. We are uneasy with poetry or contradiction, what is beyond the rational.'[5] We fear the language of the soul.

As adolescence can be a turbulent time for both parents and their children, the school has a very important support role to play in helping families to navigate these difficult waters. By assisting parents to exercise consistent controls, to formulate clear rules and expectations, to be both reasonable and accountable, schools can teach families to be authoritative, not authoritarian.

This challenge is well captured by John Harriott when he says, 'You cannot force plants to grow – only create the best conditions in which they can grow. And no more can you successfully use force on people. The use of force always marks a failure. A failure of imagination, of ingenuity, of love, of forgiveness.'[6]

The Irish have the custom of burying warm coals in the ashes at night in order to preserve the fire for the cold morning to come. Instead of cleaning out the cold hearth, people preserve yesterday's glowing coals under beds of ash overnight in order to have a fast-starting fire the next day. Those of us in school, working with the parents at home,

---

[4] Caroline Jones in 'Opinion', *The Australian*, Easter, 1996.
[5] ibid.
[6] John Harriott, *The Empire of the Heart*, Templegate, Illinois, 1990, p. 61.

are the keepers of the coals. It is up to our graduates to ensure that they fan those coals into a fire of great warmth and light in their world of the future.

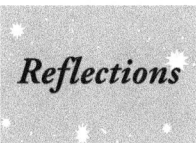

Success

Success is speaking
Words of praise
In cheering other people's ways,
In doing just the best you can
With every task and every plan.
It's silence when your
Speech would hurt,
Politeness when your
Neighbor's curt.
It's deafness when the
Scandal flows,
And sympathy with
Others' woes.
It's loyalty when duty calls.
It's courage when disaster falls.
It's found in laughter
And in song
It's in the silent time of prayer
In happiness and in despair.
In all of life and nothing less
We find the thing
We call success.

Author unknown

Failure

Failure is not the worst thing in the world. The very worst is not to try.
    Theme for a school assembly 17 April 1996

The fastest way to succeed is to double your failure rate.
    Thomas Watson, IBM

You must learn to fail intelligently. Failing is one of the greatest arts in the world. One fails forward toward success
    Thomas Edison

Success

> To laugh often and much;
> to win the respect of intelligent people
>   and the affection of children;
> to earn the appreciation of honest critics
>   and endure the betrayal of false friends;
> to appreciate beauty;
> to find the best in others;
> to leave the world a bit better,
>   whether by a healthy child,
>   a garden patch
>   or a redeemed social condition;
> to know even one life has breathed easier
>   because you have lived …
> This is to have succeeded.

attributed to Ralph Waldo Emerson

St John on success and failure

This gospel story is interesting because of what it doesn't say. The real story is often behind the text. Jesus is tired and hot. It's midday. The well is the place where the women go very early to get the water for the household for the day.

Carrying water is heavy work. The cool of dawn is the only time to do it. So why is she there at the hottest time of the day? And why is this woman so shocked that Jesus speaks to her, let alone asks for a drink?

She's there because that's the only time she can go without being picked on. She is an outcast.

First, she's a Samaritan, and Jews and Samaritans are enemies, so anyone Jewish would treat her with contempt. Second, she has broken the law. She has left her first husband and has been with a number of men since. She is living outside the law. She is suffering because she is not accepted by the others. She is an outcast.

When Jesus speaks to her she is shocked. Men do not speak to women in this society, especially Samaritan women. Jesus is quite clearly a Jew. Jesus asks her for a favour.

This short encounter changes the woman's life forever. She is given courage. She speaks to the other people in the town about this stranger who knew everything about her, who spoke gently with her, who offered her a new way of living.

This new beginning happens when she least expects it – and we can do this to others as well. By saying 'hello' to people when we pass them in the corridor, or by befriending a new boy to the school, we can give them a new beginning which could shape their life. The chance to change direction happened to this woman because she was able to reflect with honesty on her situation; she is able to see her faults, and is willing to take the risk and change her attitude.

We are all deeply hurt at times. We have all experienced times when we are shunned by others. We all have our secret insecurities or failings that we try to hide from this world. Constantly we are frightened to take a risk because we might get picked on or we might fail. But the truth is that we need to fail in order to truly succeed.

The story of Jesus and the Samaritan woman is found in John's Gospel, chapter 4.

Success and getting up again

Success does not consist
in not failing, so much as
in continually getting up.
It's all in the getting up, or
more precisely in the
gentle way in which we
get off the ground to start
again, sorry for having
failed but not surprised.

Success and risk

When you're skating on thin ice you
might as well tap dance,
stick your neck out,
volunteer,
have a go,
reach out beyond your best performance.
And when you do,
do so with style,
élan,
panache.
You will learn more
from a brilliantly executed failure

than from a success planned with
the dreary safety of what you already know.
Winning easy is boring, pointless work.

Bryce Courtenay, *A Recipe for Dreaming*, 1994

Success and humility

This is an excerpt from Professor Oliver McDonagh's speech as Guest of Honour at the 1998 Year 12 Valete and Prize-Giving Assembly at St Ignatius' College, Riverview. Professor McDonagh, himself a graduate of a Jesuit school in Ireland, had a distinguished career as a historian. His grandson graduated on this occasion, winning the highest student award, the Insignis gold medal.

When the Jesuit poet, Gerard Manley Hopkins, set out to celebrate a Jesuit saint – and there are scores – he did not choose one with a glittering career or one showered with the whole world's praise. Hopkins did not deny the splendour of the achievers. He too acclaimed the winners of the prizes. 'Honour is flashed off exploit', he wrote. But it was someone quite different who he selected as his most special person.

For his only sonnet to a saint, Hopkins chose Alphonsus Rodriguez, a Jesuit lay-brother who served forty years as doorkeeper at the order's Palma College in Majorca – and nothing more. The closing lines of Hopkins' poem ('In honour of St Alphonsus Rodriguez, Laybrother of the Society of Jesus') should bring home to all of us that, wonderful though this day may be for Riverview and its Year 12 champions, there are also quiet, unseen but much greater, glories of another sort:

> Yet God (that hews mountain and continent,
> Earth, all, out; who, with trickling increment,
> Veins violets and tall trees makes more and more)
> Could crowd career with conquest while there went
> Those years and years by of world without event
> That in Majorca Alfonso watched the door.

'Champions don't always win'

Just prior to the 2002 Head of the River, the Riverview Foundation hosted a luncheon in the Ramsay Hall to celebrate the Year of the Outback. The guest of honor was great Australian Country singer, John Williamson, who sang several very moving songs for us. I am very grateful to one of our parents who bought me a copy of his CD, *Anthems*, which contains some of the songs he sang for us that day. One of them is entitled 'A Number on My Back', known also as 'The Wallaby Anthem'. The last stanza of that song has the words:

> And if the ball won't roll my way,
> No matter how I try that day,
> I won't let my temper fray.
> I'll fight on 'til the end
> And I will keep a solid chin
> 'Cause champions don't always win.
> They're known for coming back again
> And we will make amends.

'Viewpoint', 5 April 2002

Success and God

Asked whether he prayed to win before a match, Wayne Bennett quipped: 'Sometimes at Mass I think I should pray to win. Then I feel I am seeking an unfair advantage when there are more important things than a football game. If we prepare for the game, if we do our best, he'll look after us.'

Bennett is a man of very strong commitments. 'When I got married, I wanted it to be with someone I would spend the rest of my life with. Marriage is no different from anything else I've done– you can't take it for granted. There is a commitment involved.

At weddings I refuse to give advice to the bride and groom because I'm still working at it myself ... I could have all the accolades of being what I am, but to fail in my marriage would be my greatest disappointment.'

Bennett is also someone with great common sense and balance. Of the Broncos he has said: 'The issue was not that we did not win the [1994] premiership; it was that we did not perform as well as we should have with the talent in the team. And that's what we have to rectify.'

Asked about Queensland's chances in the State of Origin, he said: 'the opportunities are there. We'll do the best we can in preparation. Everything will be spot on ...' After that? 'It's up to God.'

Wayne Bennett, Coach of the Brisbane Broncos Rugby League team. From an interview in Michael McGirr's book, *The Good Life*, Aurora/David Lovell Publishing, 2000

Success and winning?

Some time ago I read a story of the 1968 Special Olympics Track and Field Meeting. One participant was Kim Peek, a brain-damaged, severely handicapped boy racing in the 50-yard dash. Kim was racing against two other athletes with cerebral palsy. They were in wheelchairs; Kim was the lone runner.

As the gun sounded, Kim moved quickly ahead of the other two. Twenty yards ahead and ten yards from the finish line, he turned to see how the others were coming. The girl had turned her wheel chair around and was stuck against the wall. The other boy was pushing his wheel chair backwards with his feet. Kim stopped, went back and pushed the little girl across the finish line. The boy in the wheelchair going backwards won the race. The girl took second.

Kim lost. Or did he? The crowd that gave Kim a standing ovation didn't think so.

School Assembly, 1 September 2000

Success and losing?

Yesterday I was reading about the difference between success and winning. They are not the same thing. Success is being able to perform to your best – give something like 100 per cent – whether it brings a win or a loss. Often people win and are not successful. Often people lose and perform at their best and are every bit successful … What is failure? For Ignatius, after the disastrous Battle of Pamplona, it was the opportunity, the platform to create success. Failure is just a momentary stumbling. Think about how you learnt to ride a skate board – it is by getting up every time you fell down. So it was with Ignatius.

Many years ago a young man drifted through his teen years and then into his 20s. When he hit 31, he thought, 'I'd better get myself going and do something!' He formed a partnership, went into business, but in 18 months was bankrupt. Then he decided that since he was broke anyway, he'd go into politics.

At his first local election he lost badly. Two years later, aged 34, he went back into business. Bankruptcy again followed. A year later he thought things were improving when he met and fell in love with a lovely woman. She died. At 36 he suffered a nervous breakdown and was confined to bed for six months. He recovered, went back into politics, running for another local government post. He lost again. He started another business with a little more success. So at 43, he decided to run for the US Congress. He lost. At 46 he ran for Congress again, and he lost again. At 48 he ran for the Senate and lost that as well. When he was 55, he tried for his party's nomination for Vice-President. He was badly defeated. At age 58 he ran for the Senate again, and again he lost.

Finally, at 60 years of age, Abraham Lincoln was elected to his first public office – President of the United States of America.

Failure is only a temporary setback. It is an opportunity to go forward to achieve success. Confucius once said that 'our greatest glory is not in never falling, but in rising every time we fall.'

School Assembly, 26 August 1998

Living in the present

Lift your eyes and look. Who made these stars, i not he who drills them like an army, calling each one by name?

Isaiah 40:26

Given the frenetic busyness of schools when in session, I suppose it is only natural that many of us tend to live from one school holiday to the next. Teachers live in anticipation of the vacations, while parents enjoy the prospect of school returning to term time. Nonetheless, if both of us are not careful we could spend our time wishing our lives away, concentrating on the bookends of past and future and neglecting the rich present stacked between them.

Many readers would remember the wonderfully colourful television coverage of the fireworks display on Sydney Harbour on the eve of the third millennium. While it was exciting and spectacularly beautiful, I was particularly struck by the one word illuminated on the eastern face of the bridge – 'Eternity'.

For many years around Sydney, an enigmatic born-again Christian named Arthur Stace would travel all over the city, and sometimes as far as Newcastle and Wollongong, writing in coloured chalk the word 'Eternity' in the elegant script visible on the bridge that night. One could find it on footpaths, in subways; indeed, the last surviving sample is inscribed inside the largest bell of Sydney's old GPO bell tower on Martin Place. His identity remained a mystery for some 26 years until it was discovered in 1956.

The director of the New Year celebrations in Sydney that night was Ignatius Jones, a very colourful graduate of St Ignatius' College, and it was his brainchild to have the word 'Eternity' as the focus of the celebrations. He gave his reasons as follows:

> It's incredibly, Sydney. It symbolized for me the madness, mystery and magic of the city. On the one hand there's the meaning of the word in its temporal sense – and on this night of fellowship and good cheer, it shouldn't just be about one night. The word says that this celebration should be eternal in human life.
>
> But it also says a lot about Sydney that Arthur Stace, who grew up in a brothel, came back from war shell-shocked and became a habitual criminal and an alcoholic, should be able to reinvent himself and try to bring joy and meaning into people's lives.[1]

This story is valuable because it captures succinctly what we staff and parents are trying to achieve with young people in schools. I am very fond of the statement by Dr Jonathan Sacks, when speaking about the importance of religious education in schools. He said, 'You defend a country by armies. But you defend a civilization by schools.' In a time of social instability, children needed more than ever a sense of 'rootedness in a living tradition. We need to teach our children to hear the sound of eternity in the midst of change.'[2]

Is not that a splendid definition of our role in schools? Is it not our ministry to teach our students 'to hear the sound of eternity in the midst of change'? It is what Sebastian Moore means, when talking about

---
[1] *Sydney Morning Herald*, 1 January 2000
[2] Quoted in *The Tablet*, 9 July 1994.

the resurrection, that 'the virus of eternity has entered our bloodstream for ever.'³ I can remember hearing a BBC interview with three heads of schools regarding their philosophy of education. The first two said the sorts of things we write in our glossy prospectuses and brochures. But when it came to the Headmaster of Ampleforth, a Benedictine priest, he made the show-stopping comment: 'In our school, we prepare boys for death.' Is that not the same as teaching them to hear the sound of eternity? As the *Sydney Morning Herald* editorial said so well: 'Life is a dry run for Eternity.'

While listening recently to a radio discussion about Time, I heard a newly published author make a word-play on an old song: 'We're all wild about hurry.' He was reflecting critically on the faster pace with which we are called to run our lives now, making mention of the latest absurdity in publications – 'Thirty Second Bedtime Stories' – for parents to read to their children before bed. He was asking the question: is faster better? At the end of the interview he proffered his own thesis that the fast pace of life for so many is driven by a fear of being alone, a fear of death.

Like many precious commodities, the gift of time is difficult to handle. Sometimes we have too much of it, more often too little. Frequently we can hanker after the past or dwell on it excessively – so much so that we forget that life is to be savoured and enjoyed in the present. Similarly, we can wish our short lives away so quickly that we live always for the future and miss out on the beauties of the present time. We need to be reminded that there is a place of rest in our lives, 'a place where we must be if we are to function well. This place of resting – the arms of God, if you will – is simply here and now: seeing, hearing, touching, smelling, tasting our life as it is.'⁴

---

³ Sebastian Moore, *Jesus the Liberator of Desire*, New York, 1989, p. 57.
⁴ Zen teacher, Charlotte Joto Beck, in Stephanie Dowrick, *Forgiveness and Other Acts of Love: Finding True Value in Your Life*, Penguin, Australia, 1997, p. 332.

It was fascinating as a religious person to hear on national radio, not so long ago, a guest speaker on the afternoon 'Drive Time' show talking about God 'winking at you' during the day. Petria King was making the point that one of the great blessings of our body is that it is always in the present, in the world of what is. If one believes in God, the present is where God can be found.

The mind, on the other hand, with its endless inner commentary, tries to take us off into the future, into the world of what isn't. Creativity is a present-time activity, and if we are absent from the present we sacrifice the following four qualities of our lives: our spontaneity, our humour, our creativity, and our self-confidence. God is certainly to be found in the creative, and the only moment for that discovery is the present.

Over the past few years in December we offered at Riverview the Ignatian Children's Holiday Camp to over 100 young people who are severely handicapped. It is a four day live-in experience using all the facilities at school for some 30 children at a time. The carers are senior students who must apply for the position and pass an interview for this demanding role of looking after some very dependent and demanding children 24 hours a day. Many staff and parents also volunteer to give their time generously to this program. Indeed, when I read the following letter of a parent writing to thank the College for the holiday enjoyed by her son and their family, I understood afresh how time is a great gift.

> Our son has just spent four of the most wonderful days
> of his life …
> We haven't seen him that happy for a long time …
> During the Christmas party a spokesman took the microphone
> And thanked all of the staff,
> The nurses,
> The caterers,
> And of course the tremendous young adults

Whose responsibility it was to ensure
All of our children enjoyed themselves.
He also thanked us the parents for allowing
The students and staff
Those four days to look after our special children …
It was a humbling experience.
However, it didn't feel right,
Because we parents couldn't thank you
For such a wonderful gift to us …
I wanted to scream from the rooftops,
Thank you!
The generosity of this camp gave our son
Not just a wonderful time
But the most precious gift of all to my wife and me –
The gift of time.
It was a time for us to just appreciate the
Quiet of our house,
The ability to sleep
And not to have to hear
'Mum' or 'Dad' spoken so constantly –
It drives you batty …
You have done a wonderful thing.

Another perspective on time comes from the Jesuit tradition and is contained in the story of a conversation between the Founder, Ignatius Loyola, and one of his key lieutenants, Diego Lainez. It goes like this:

> Ignatius: Tell me, Master Lainez, what do you think you would do, were God our Lord to say, 'If you want to die soon, I will release you from the prison of this body and give you eternal glory. If you prefer to stay alive, I give you no assurance as to what will become of you'? If our Lord told you this, and you thought that by remaining for some time in this life you could render some outstanding service to his Divine Majesty, which would you choose?

> Lainez: I must confess, Father, I would choose to go soon to enjoy God and to assure my salvation and to avoid the perils in so important a matter.
> Ignatius: I certainly would not. If I thought that by remaining in this life I could render some single service to our Lord, I would beg him to leave me here until I had done it, and I would not think twice of the peril to me or the assurance of my salvation.[5]

For me this is a very powerful story about time. Commenting on this conversation, Ross Jones SJ, in his homily to Australian Jesuit school administrators in March 1995, said:

> In an age when God was, for the most part, perceived as a harsh judge, when damnation was an ever-present possibility, it takes a courageous man to opt for the last chance of service in this world, even though it might be at the cost of his soul. I wonder what our reply might be were God to say to us today, 'You can come to heaven now, or I'll leave you in the school one more year'? For Ignatius, the world was 'user-friendly'. God is there in the guise of humanity. Discovered in service. Gracing our way. Worth the risk of discovering. Yet in the microcosm of the school, in its business and struggles, oft time the face of God is in heavy disguise. We know service can be hard. Nature may readily gain the upper hand on grace. But, I take heart in a phrase I learned from one of my staff – Young people are the promise of tomorrow, a blessing for today. For them I think I'd happily stand alongside Ignatius in this present reality. Maybe even risk heaven in the endeavour.

The great US statesman and Secretary of State, Dean Acheson once said that 'the best thing about the future is that it only comes one day at a time'. Living in the present, therefore, is crucial for developing a quality of soul in our lives and in the lives of those for whom we care.

---
[5] Pedro Ribadeneira, *Vida del bienaventurado Padre Ignatio de Loyola*, 2nd ed., Subirana, Barcelona, 1885, pp. 501-502.

In some ways, the present is the only time that young people know and about which they are concerned. Yet we have much to teach them about being present in the present, being aware and reflective about what is going on inside and outside themselves, ensuring that life does not simply wash over them like some huge wave.

Eckhart Tolle captures these sentiments beautifully:

> The more you are focused on time – past and future – the more you miss the Now, the most precious thing there is. Why is it the most precious thing? Firstly, because it is the only thing. It's all there is. The eternal present is the space within which your whole life unfolds, the one factor that remains constant. Life is now. There was never a time when your life was not now, nor will there ever be. Secondly, the Now is the only point that can take you beyond the limited confines of the mind. It is your only point of access into the timeless and formless realm of Being.[6]

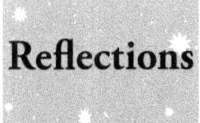

Reflections

God's today

Don't let yourself be torn
between yesterday
and tomorrow.
Live always and only
God's today.

Dom Helder Camara, *A Thousand Reasons for Living*, 1984, p. 75

---

[6] Eckhart Tolle, *The Power of Now: A Guide to Spiritual Enlightenment*, New World Library, 1998.

> Accept surprises
> that upset your plans,
> shatter your dreams,
> give a completely
> different turn
> to your day
> and – who knows? –
> to your life.
> It is not chance.
> Leave the Father free
> Himself to weave
> The pattern of your days.
>
> Dom Helder Camara, *A Thousand Reasons for Living*, 1984, p. 92

Living in the moment

Ann Morrow Lindbergh likens a good relationship to a good dance, for it is, in her words:

> … built on the same rules. The partners do not need to hold on tightly, because they move confidently in the same pattern … To touch heavily would be to arrest the pattern and freeze the movement … There is no place here for the possessive clutch, the clinging arm, the heavy hand; only the barest touch in passing. Now arm in arm, now face to face, now back to back – it does not matter which. Because they know they are partners moving to the same rhythm, creating a pattern is not only the joy of creation or the joy of participation, it is also the joy of living in the moment. Lightness of touch and living in the moment are intertwined. One cannot dance well unless one is completely in time with the music, not leaning back to the last step or pressing forward to the next one, but poised directly on the present step as it comes.

Perfect poise on the beat is what gives good dancing its sense of ease, of timelessness, of the eternal.
Anne Morrow, *Gift from the Sea*, Pantheon, 1983, pp. 104-105.

Four things come not back – the spoken word, the sped arrow, the past life, and the neglected opportunity.
Arabian proverb

Heaven

Once we turn away from childish notions of heaven, we find it where it has always been – inside ourselves. Because God is, heaven is – like God – everywhere. A disappointed disciple, the Talmud teaches, seeing studious rabbis pouring over the Torah in a plain anteroom of heaven, asks of the angel who is conducting him through paradise, 'Are those sages in heaven?' And the angel answers him, 'Oh, no, friend. The sages are not in heaven. Heaven is in the sages.'
Joan Chittister, *In Search of Belief*, Ligouri, 1999, p. 50.

The present

Today is a gift, that is why we call it the present.
Right now,
somebody is very proud of you;
somebody is thinking of you;
somebody is caring about you;
somebody misses you;
somebody hopes you are not in trouble;
somebody is thankful for the support you have provided;
somebody wants you to be happy.
School Assembly, 23 May 2002

'Exult in the process.' This was the challenge extended by the 2001 Dux of the School, Robert McMonnies, to the School Assembly in February 2002.

Take time

Take time to rest – it is the foundation of health and vitality.
Take time to think – it is the source of achievement.
Take time to read – it is the foundation of wisdom.
Take time to play – it is the secret of staying young.
Take time to be quiet – it is the opportunity to seek God.
Take time to share – it is too short a life to be selfish.
Take time to be aware – it is the opportunity to help others.
Take time to laugh – it's the music of the heart.
Take time to be loved – it nourishes the soul.
Take time to be friendly – it is the road to happiness.
Take time to pray – it is the greatest power on earth.
Take time to dream – it's the well of inspiration.
There is time for everything.

> There is a season for everything,
> a time for every occupation under heaven.
> Ecclesiastes 3:1

Take the long view

It helps now and then to step back and take the long view.

The kingdom is not only beyond our efforts,
it is even beyond our vision.

We accomplish in our lifetime only a tiny fraction
of the magnificent enterprise that is God's work.

Nothing we do is complete, which is another way of saying that the kingdom always lies beyond us.

No statement says all that could be said.
No prayer fully expresses our faith.
No confession brings perfection.
No pastoral visit brings wholeness.
No program accomplishes the church's mission.
No set of goals and objectives includes everything.

This is what we are about.

We plant the seeds that one day will grow.
We water seeds already planted,
Knowing that they hold future promise.
We lay foundations that will need further development.
We provide yeast that produces
Far beyond our capabilities.

We cannot do everything,
and there is a sense of liberation in realizing that.
This enables us to do something, and to do it well,

It may be incomplete, but it is a beginning,
A step along the way,
an opportunity for the Lord's grace to enter
and do the rest.
We may never see the end results,
But that is the difference
between the master builder and the worker.

We are workers, not master builders
ministers, not messiahs.
We are prophets of a future
not our own.

Archbishop Oscar Romero

What then?

The story is told of the young man who went to visit William Gladstone who served as Prime Minister of Great Britain from 1868 to 1874. The young man told Mr Gladstone that he would like to study law. 'Yes', said the Prime Minister, 'and what then?'

'Then I would like to serve in Parliament in the House of Lords', the young man smiled. 'Yes', Gladstone said, 'and what then?'

'Well', the young man replied, getting a bit uncomfortable with Gladstone's What thens?, 'I suppose I will die.'

'Yes', said Gladstone soberly. 'What then?'

'I have no plans beyond that', the young man replied. 'I have never thought any further than that.'

'Then', Gladstone sternly replied, 'young man, you are a fool. You need to go home and think life through.'

Being available

If you could change one thing to improve the lives of the rising generation of young Australians, and to increase their chances of finding happiness in an unstable world, what would it be?

Would you banish drugs from the dance scene? (Good luck.) Would you insist they all learn a foreign language or a musical instrument, or that they acquire sophisticated computer skills? Would you make team sport compulsory in every school? Would you reintroduce national service training – either military service (which the defence forces would hate), or community service, here or overseas? Would you encourage a return to religion, en masse? (Watch it; you could find yourself in a fine fundamentalist pickle of prohibition, regulation, stricture and sobriety.)

My answer, for what it's worth, would be none of the above. I'd change the parents. I'd want them to be more available to their offspring and, at the same time, more relaxed.

Forgive this outbreak of gratuitous advice, but it arose from a question I was asked at a meeting of high-school parents who were concerned about giving their teenage offspring the best possible start in life. In a nutshell, my suggestion was this: be there more, and try less hard.

I'd urge parents to wash their mouths out every time they uttered those high-pressure words 'quality time'. With so many parents running such tight schedules, it's tempting to feel that when you are available to your kids, every minute has to count. But moments of intimacy between parent and child are fleeting, at best, and they can't be programmed. They generally occur simply because you happened to be there at the moment when someone wanted to know how to spell 'parallel', or suddenly thought to mention that they'd had a detention today, or wondered how best to discourage an unwanted admirer.

Our absence at such moments – or our half-hearted presence, when we're too stressed or distracted to give our undivided attention – sends the implicit message that we are more concerned about ourselves than our children.

Firstly, I'd put more emphasis on 'hanging-around time', because that's the only time that really counts. The big thing is simply to be there as much as you can, being yourself, getting on with your own stuff, just in case you are needed for a spot of advice, as a listening post, or even as a vaguely irritating but curiously reassuring presence in the background.

But being there is only half the story. Equally important is the need to back off, to be less earnest, to refrain from over-zealous displays of interest in your teenager's life. Your offspring want you to be interested in them when they want you to be interested in them, not when you want to be interested in them. And don't try to pick the moment.

One of a parent's most unsettling experiences is to hear children declaring their intention to be better parents than their own parents have been. When it happens, it's as well to remember that we probably once made the same declaration ourselves; parents often report that they handle parenting better than their own parents did – more conscientious, more sensitive, more focused.

It might even be true. Each generation is becoming better educated about the psychology of parenting and the business of managing relationships. But perhaps each generation of parents simply makes a new set of mistakes.

Certainly, when you listen to today's teenagers criticizing their hapless parents, there's a common theme: Why don't they back off? Why are they so interested in everything? Why are they always up at the school? Why are they so involved in my life?

This is heartbreak stuff, because it reflects the desire of many members of the present generation of parents to stay close to their teenage children (and even, misguidedly, to be their children's best friends). But if the parents' job is to prepare their children for independence, staying too close is bound to undermine the process.

Nowhere is that more evident than in the parents' reluctance to give their children space for the development of self-discipline, and even for the experience of failure. Many middle-class teenagers, in particular, report that their parents' stifling concern (especially about schoolwork) is the greatest source of stress in their lives.

Unhappily, the very keenness of some parents, and their ferocious determination to be 'good parents', can blind them to their teenagers' need for acceptance, support, encouragement ... all delivered from a safe distance, of course, and with the lips scarcely moving.

From social researcher, Hugh Mackay, in the *Sydney Morning Herald*, 11 March 2000

Take time

Take time off each day to think and pray,
To care how your life is going.
Give your roots rain.

Take time with a friend to do nothing too important,
But just be together, to enjoy another person.
Give your roots rain.

Take time to write a poem or grow a flower,
To create something that is something of you.
Give your roots rain.

For in your roots you find who you are,
And there too you find who God is,
For he has not forced you into his home,
Rather he has made his home in you.

When our time runs out

Cardinal Wolsey was a great achiever. From fairly humble beginnings he rose to be Lord Chancellor of England, one of the most powerful positions in the country. He owed it all to his lord and master, King Henry VIII, to whom he gave unswerving loyalty. In the end he fell out of favour and finished back where he started.

When he came to die, he uttered those immortal words for which he is most remembered: 'Would that I had served my God but half as well as I had served my King.'

What started me thinking about this was something I had been reading recently in the paper. It was a column devoted to young and highly successful entrepreneurs who had risen to the top in their various business fields. It related to their lifestyle.

They were asked questions like, 'What make of car do you drive?' They all drove top of the range models. 'What is your favourite restaurant?' Again it was only the best.

The answers to the last question were the most revealing. The question was, 'What do you think your last words on earth will be?' Some typical answers were: 'Can I do it all again?' 'What, is it that time already?' 'It was good while it lasted.'

It made me wonder what the rest of us would have to say if we were told that in a short space of time we would be coming face-to-face with God.

Jack Quinn

One day at a time

There are two days in every week we should not worry about.
Two days which should be kept free from fear and
    apprehension.

One of these days is Yesterday with its mistakes and cares,
its faults and blunders, its aches and pains.
Yesterday has passed forever beyond our control.
All the money in the world cannot bring back yesterday.
We cannot undo a single act we performed;
we cannot erase a single word we said.
Yesterday is gone forever.

The other day we should not worry about is Tomorrow,
With all its possible adversities, its burdens,
its large promise and poor performance.
Tomorrow is also beyond our immediate control.
Tomorrow's sun will rise,
either in splendour or behind a mask of clouds, but it will rise.
Until it does, we have no stake in tomorrow, for it is yet
    unborn.

This just leaves only one day – Today.
Any person can fight the battles of just one day.
It is only when you and I add the burdens of those two awful
eternities – Yesterday and tomorrow – that we break down.

It is not the experience of today that drives people mad.
It is the remorse or bitterness for something
which happened yesterday
and the dread of what tomorrow may bring.

Let us therefore live but one day at a time.

Author unknown

Being people of our time

There are times when the world's problems seem too much. But Ignatius loved to look up in wonder at night at the stars and contemplate the grandeur of the created and the creator, meditating on the creature and the creator in himself and in each of us. I have returned to Sydney to find the city stopped in wonder at the vision of three whales playing under the Harbour Bridge. We live in such a fast, non-religious society, but here we all are gazing in wonder, celebrating the transcendent as we behold the gift of life in its enormity and grace splashing about in the water.

Like Ignatius who was a man of his time, each of us is called to be a person of our time confident in faith that there is a time for every purpose under heaven.'

From the homily by Father Frank Brennan sj on the Feast of St Ignatius of Loyola, 31 July 2002

Falling in love with the present

I shall pass through this world but once.
If, therefore, there be any kindness I can show,
Or any good thing I can do,
Let me not defer it, nor neglect it,
For I may not pass this way again.

Author unknown

Say goodbye
to golden yesterdays
– or your heart
will never learn
to love
the present.

Anthony de Mello sj, *Hearts on Fire: Praying with Jesuits*, Michael Harter sj (ed), p. 33.

'When you cannot have what you think you would enjoy, you must learn to enjoy what you have or you will wish your life away while roses die at your feet.'

Joan Chittister, *Songs of Joy*, p. 108, entry for 11 September

The richness of the instant
Dogs and God

That bikie with his
girl as pillion,
that kelpie in his

sidecar there
singing in the wind
The girl with blonde hair

blowing back
is smiling sidelong
at the dog

who measures in his
cancelled song
the richness of the instant

And who among you
cruising by
would still deny

the fact of heaven?
If dogs have souls
and God's tattooed

and every angel
has blonde hair
streaming from a helmet

Geoff Page

'Spectrum', *Sydney Morning Herald*, 9-10 March 2002

Living with the Maker of the Stars

> *The best description I know of the Dakota sky came from a little girl at an elementary school on the Minot Air Force Base, a shy black girl who had recently moved from Louisiana and seemed overwhelmed by her new environment. She wrote: 'The sky is full of blue / and full of the mind of God.'*
> **Kathleen Norris,** *Dakota: A Spiritual Geography*, **2001**

In Salisbury Cathedral one can find the following reflection: 'Lighting a candle is a prayer. When we have gone it stays alight, kindling in the hearts and minds of others the prayers we have already offered for them and for others.' Prayer is an affair of the heart, a familiarity with God. Just as the soul is that part of a person which is God, or reflects God, so prayer is food for the soul. If we imagine that the soul is a candle, God might be seen as its huge flame. Prayer is the lighting of this candle and spirituality is the keeping alight of this inner flame, fanning it, appreciating its colors and warmth, allowing air and space around it so that it can stay alight.

When St Ignatius founded the Society of Jesus in 1540, he wanted his followers to have a spirituality appropriate for people on the move, ever ready and flexible to respond to the hurch's needs anywhere and at any time. Not tied to worshipping God in a monastery like the older religious orders, the Jesuits were called by Ignatius to focus their lives on 'finding God in all things'. This was to be the centrepiece of their spirituality, a tradition I have inherited as a Jesuit and share with so many people across the globe, and one which weaves its seamless way through this chapter.

Contemporaries of Ignatius, like his secretary Father Juan Polanco, understood and caught this spirit. In a letter he wrote to Father Urban Fernandes in 1551, Polanco counsels:

> It is better to devote oneself to finding God in everything, than that one should spend a long time in prayer. And the spirit that our Father Ignatius desires to find in members of the Society is that, if possible, they find no less devotion in works of charity and obedience than in prayer and meditation. As a matter of fact, they should do nothing except for the love and service of God our Lord.

As mentioned elsewhere in this book, Ignatius saw the world as very 'user-friendly'. For him, every part of it, from the stars in the heavens to the flowers of the field, elevated his mind and heart to God. In Ribadeneira's *Life of Ignatius* we learn 'how even the smallest things could make his spirit soar upwards to God, who even in the smallest things is Greatest. At the sight of a little plant, a leaf, a flower or a fruit, an insignificant worm or a tiny animal Ignatius could soar free above the heavens and reach through into things which lie beyond the senses, (*Life*, III 5381).

The centenary book for the foundation of the Society of Jesus, *Imago primi saeculi* (1640), contains a Latin maxim composed by an unknown Flemish Jesuit scholastic, which has come to be called 'Loyola's Epitaph': *Non coerceri maximo, contineri tamen a minimo divinum est* – 'Not to be encompassed by the greatest, yet to let oneself be encompassed by the tiniest – that is the mark of divinity.'

We have seen how nature lifted Ignatius' mind to God. Indeed, Father Jeronimo Nadal says that he saw the Trinity in the leaf of an orange tree. Ignatius would have resonated easily with the Hindu image of God the Dancer in the dance of creation. Anthony de Mello elaborates:

> The dance is different from the Dancer, and yet it has no existence apart from Him ... Be silent and contemplate the Dance. Just look: a star, a flower, a fading leaf, a bird, a stone ... any fragment of the Dance will do.
> Look. Listen. Smell. Touch. Taste.
> And, hopefully, it won't be long before you see God. It won't be long before you see the Dancer in person![1]

Seeking and finding God in all things works on the belief that God is already present in our world and it is our task to uncover his presence and help others to do the same. It is very different to the old, perhaps arrogant, concept of ministry which talked about 'bringing God to the world'. As the famous Jesuit theologian Karl Rahner said so well: 'The grace of God has always been there ahead of our preaching ... Hence our preaching is not really an indoctrination with something alien from outside, but the awakening of something within, as yet not understood but nevertheless really present.' [2] Finding God in all things is also a matter of being found by God in all things, allowing the Hound of Heaven of Psalm 139, who knows us intimately from our mother's womb, to seek us out and provide for us.

There is a very interesting video entitled *Interview with God*[3] in which God is depicted as expressing surprise that humans are so worried and anxious about the future that they forget the present and consequently live in neither the present nor the future. A familiar theme? God also expresses surprise in the video that we humans get bored with childhood, rush to grow up, and then long to be children again. I can

---

[1] Anthony de Mello sj, *The Song of the Bird*, Gujarat, 1982, p. 16.
[2] Karl Rahner, 'On the Significance in Redemptive History of the Individual Member of the Church', *Mission and Grace*, 1963, p. 156.
[3] See the website http.//www.theinterviewwithgod.com.

remember Anthony de Mello telling us that in every adult there is a deteriorated child. One of the great qualities of the child is his or her power of imagination and one of the weaknesses in our religious quests and spiritual journeys today is a failure or deficiency in imagination. Cardinal John Henry Newman argued this over a century ago: '… the heart is commonly reached, not through the reason, but through the imagination.' Belief in God, he says, originates in our imagination, not in ideas. The real battles of life take place within the imagination.

Some seven-year-olds from Eastwood in Sydney, when asked to describe what elements in nature reminded them of God, exercised their fertile imaginations to produce the following:

> The seed reminds me of God because it grows gently and looks for the sun, like God searches for people in need, and it never means to hurt someone.
>
> The rainforest reminds me of God because it provides food and helps all sorts of things grow and everything in the rainforest is as happy as can be that way and that will hopefully stay the same for the rest of time we are alive and even longer.
>
> God is like a fire because it stays alight for a long time and it runs by sticks, like God runs by hope, love, safety, life and gracefulness, plus much more.
>
> The butterflies remind me of God because they are like little angels and angels flutter peacefully and I think that God is very peaceful.
>
> The waterfall reminds me of God because God never stops working either so God never turns away from us even for one second.
>
> God is like the sprinkling rain because he is soft and gentle and he never goes too hard on us.

The rose reminds me of God because it is fragile and if you hurt the rose you will hurt God too. He's perfect because he's a perfect rose.

The stream reminds me of God because God never stops or leaves it half finished. He always finishes it – God keeps on going not stopping till it is all finished.

God is like the ocean because sometimes he's calm and gentle or strong and mighty.

God is like the storms because they are mighty and undefeatable, and God is exactly like that – mighty and undefeatable. When storms are raining heavily, God is love. [4]

The power of children's imagination gives them a very rich imagery about God as the following very personal letters attest:

'Dear God, I do not think that anybody could be a better God. Well I just want you to know but I am not just saying that because you are God.' Charles.

'Dear God, I didn't think orange went with purple until I saw the sunset you made on Tue. That was cool.' Eugene.

'Dear God, It is great the way you get the stars in the right places.' Jeff.

'Dear God, if you watch in church on Sunday I will show you my new shoes.' Mickey D.

'Dear God, I bet it is very hard for you to love all of everybody in the whole world. There are only four people in our family and I can never do it.' Nan.

---

[4] Kevin Bates SM, 'Nurturing Our Children's Faith', from his web site www.kevinfbates.com

'Dear God, Thank you for the baby brother but what I prayed for was a puppy.' Joyce. [5]

W. H. Auden once wrote: 'To pray is to pay attention to something or someone other than oneself. Whenever a man so concentrates his attention – on a landscape, a poem, a geometrical problem, an idol, or the True God – that he completely forgets his own ego and desires, he is praying.' Good literature has this capacity to elevate or stretch us towards God as captured in the magnificent perspective on literature offered by C. S. Lewis:

> Literature enlarges our being by admitting us to experiences not our own. They may be beautiful, terrible, awe-inspiring, exhilarating, pathetic, comic, or merely piquant. Literature gives the entree to them all. Those of us who have been true readers all our life, seldom realize the enormous extension of our being that we owe to authors ... In reading great literature, I become a thousand men and yet remain myself. Like the night sky in a Greek poem, I see with a thousand eyes, but it is still I who see. Here, as in worship, in love, in moral action, and in knowing, I transcend myself; and am never more myself than when I do.[6]

Yet is this self-transcendence enough in our quest to find God in the daily geography of our lives? The 2002 Lenten Series of articles written by the American Franciscan priest Richard Rohr for the *National Catholic Reporter*, was called 'Liminal Space'. Not having a clue what 'liminal space' meant, I searched the web for his first article to discover what I should have known, that 'the Latin word *limina* means threshold, from the *ad limina* visits of our [Catholic] bishops to the doorstep of Peter in Rome. Liminality is a special psychic and spiritual place "where

---

[5] *From Children's Letters to God: The New Collection*, compiled by Stuart Hample and Eric Marshall, Kyle Cathie Ltd, 1992.
[6] From Pierre Ryckmans, 'The View From the Bridge: Aspects of Culture', 1996 Boyer Lectures, Lecture 3.

all transformation happens". It is when we are betwixt and between, and therefore by definition "not in control". Nothing new happens as long as we are inside our self-constructed comfort zone. Nothing good or creative emerges from business as usual' (*National Catholic Reporter*, 1 February 2002). Transformation has far more impact on us in our quest for God than does transcendence.

This began to ring a few bells for me. Early in 2002 I received a transcript of a Radio National *Encounter* interview with Richard Holloway, the recently and early retired Bishop of Edinburgh. He was described in the summary as one 'who dances on the edge of his church'. Surely, I began to think, he was someone who lived on the edge, on the threshold, who occupied liminal space. In that interview, Holloway told the story of the British playwright, Dennis Potter, who was dying of cancer and was asked in a television interview whether his imminent death had brought a new religious intensity or a recovery of boyhood faith. Potter's reply was: 'Religion to me has always been the wound, not the bandage.'[7]

What Dennis Potter and Richard Holloway are both saying to us is that being in touch with our own vulnerability is a very important avenue to finding God. Irish Jesuit, Michael Paul Gallagher, makes the same point when he says, 'there are moments when each of us runs into destructive demons, and such encounters can leave us feeling shaken or fragile. Then either we retreat into normality or else we have courage to face more humbling revelations Any love relationship will sooner or later touch zones of vulnerability … But when I risk staying in touch with my weakness or fear, and, even more so, if I can communicate what I feel to another person, shadows become thresholds of transformation.'[8]

In the same chapter Gallagher goes on to talk about thresholds of

---

[7] 'Inns on Roads', *Encounter*, Radio National, 23 December 2001.
[8] Michael Paul Gallagher, *Dive Deeper: The Human Poetry of Faith*, DLT, London, 2001, p. 29.

tenderness, quoting Sebastian Barry's play *The Steward of Christendom*. The head of the Dublin City Police, now a difficult and moody old man in a home for the elderly, reflects on a threshold of tenderness in his life while waiting for his wife to deliver their youngest child. 'I started to tremble, it was a moment in your life when daily things pass away from you, when all your concerns seem to vanish, and you are allowed by God a little space of clarity and grace. When you see that God himself is in your wife and in your children, and they hold in trust for you your own measure of goodness. And in the manner of your treatment of them lies your own salvation.'[9]

In retrospect I suppose all this talk about suffering as a teacher, about the cauldron of transformation, is what moved me in a splendid article by Ruth Ostrow entitled 'Accept, and reach for the scars' in *The Weekend Australian*.[10] The author wrote about a woman she had met who had elected not to have breast reconstruction surgery after having her breast removed for cancer. Instead, she opted to live simply with her scar, even arriving at a party wearing a tight top that greatly accentuated the absence of her breast. Proud of her war wound, the woman explained:

> I feel like a warrior woman. This is the sacrifice I've made in my fight against cancer. And I like to show it off. So many of us feel we have to cover our scars, our war wounds, the signs of a life well lived, a life that has been marked by falls, and broken bones and broken hearts, smile lines, frown lines, the time we crashed our bicycle. But I think the scars we see on people are beautiful. They are our stories and our memories. They are the disasters we lived through and survived. We lived to tell another tale. And we can be more compassionate as a result of our wound. And people can approach us because we look imperfect and truthful and real.

---

[9] ibid., p. 36.
[10] *The Weekend Australian*, 5-6 January 2002.

In the same edition of *The Weekend Australian* we have Australia's well-known atheist, Phillip Adams, writing about the hereafter, or, to be more accurate, the 'thereafter' as he calls it. 'Does heaven take credit cards? Does it have valet parking? Are there trade unions? Do angels get frequent-flyer points? Is there room service? Come to think of it, do you eat in heaven?' I have always thought that Phillip Adams is what Richard Holloway calls 'a God-obsessed atheist'. He is continually placing the 'God question' before us and assisting us in our quest to 'find God in all things'. The graffitist who signed 'God' after the statement on the wall 'Nietzsche is dead' was telling us something important. Our biggest danger is never atheism, but idolatry, the creation of false gods. We are good at creating all sorts of idols like success, sport, security, and pleasure. Religion too can have its idols of 'false absolutes'.[11] We must be on the lookout lest we are tempted to make God in our own image – God who works across all religions and in the hearts of those who profess to have no religion at all.

In presenting various glimpses of God in the geography of our ordinary life, I believe that 'finding God in all things' is closely linked to all those experiences we have in life of being fully alive. After all, it was St Irenaeus who coined those famous words, 'The glory of God is a human person fully alive.'

One of my more attentive students once asked me why I always began my homilies with a story. 'Not that I mind, Father, I am just curious', he added hastily. I tried to explain that stories act as a bridge to our audience , and immediately link the listener to the speaker's experience. Stories that reveal the best qualities of the human spirit and character connect us immediately to God and tell us something about him or her.

Let me share here some of the stories I have used in talking about God to young people, their families, and school communities.

---

[11] Michael Paul Gallagher, *Struggles of Faith*, Dublin, 1991, p. 90.

God's Holy Spirit

About 25 years ago, a young Year 10 boy came home from school very upset, ran upstairs, and slammed his bedroom door. His mother followed him up there and sitting down on the bed beside him asked him what the matter was. He was really upset by now and said that he didn't make the school basketball squad because he was too small. That was the finish. There were no B or C or D teams – he was cut from the squad altogether because he was too small.

His mother was acutely aware that whatever she said to the boy then could mean the difference between success and failure for him. After pausing and thinking briefly, she said, 'Son, you can never be too small. It's not the size of the person in the game that matters, but the size of the game in the person.'

The next morning his mother heard the alarm bell go off at 4.30 am and her son going downstairs and out into the yard to start practising. From that time on he practised every morning and evening, no matter what the weather was. And as he practised, he kept repeating to himself, 'It is not the size of the player in the game that counts, but the size of the game in the player.'

Of course, when the basketball trials came round again he played with such focus and skill he made the team that year and for every year after that. He went on to become one of the great athletes of our time – I am referring, of course, to the basketballer, Michael Jordan.

Mass of the Holy Spirit, February 2002

God is found in the people who need him most

The story is told of the woman who was very religious and devout and filled with the love of God. Each morning she would go to church. And on her way children would call out to her, beggars would accost her, but so immersed was she in her devotions that she did not even see them.

One day she walked down the street in her customary manner and arrived at the church just in time for the service. She pushed the door, but it would not open. She pushed it again harder, and found the door locked.

Distressed at the thought that she would miss her religious service for the first time in years, and not knowing what to do, she looked up. And there, right before her face, she found a note pinned on the door. It said: 'I'm out there!'

Homily, 5 March 2000

We learn about God through the best qualities of our parents

The other day I read about a young boy who was consistently coming home late from school. There seemed to be no good reason for his lateness, and his father became very frustrated with him. So he sat him down one night he came home late, and warned him, 'If you come home late from school once again, you will be given bread and water for your supper – and nothing else. Is that clear?' The little boy looked straight at his father and nodded. It was perfectly clear.

A few days later the boy came home even later than usual. His mother met him at the door but didn't say anything. His father met him in the living room, but he didn't say anything either.

That night, when they sat down to dinner, the boy's heart sank when he looked at the table. His father's plate was filled with food, and so was his mother's. In front of him, however, was one lonely slice of bread and a glass of water. To make matters worse, this was a night on which he was absolutely starving.

The father waited for the full impact to sink in, then quietly took the boy's plate and placed it in front of himself. He took his own plate and put it in front of the boy.

The boy understood what his father was doing. His father was taking upon himself the punishment that he, the boy, had brought on himself by his own bad behavior. Years later, that same boy remembered this incident and said, 'All my life, I've known what God is like by what my father did that night.'

Homily at Grandparents' Day Mass, 22 September 2001

God and issues of our identity

Not many people would be brave enough to ask the question posed by Jesus in the gospel – 'Who do people say I am?' When George Bush Senior was President of the United States, he was doing his rounds of public relations in a nursing home one day. He came upon a wizened old man hobbling down the corridor. President Bush took the man by the hand and said, 'Sir, do you know who I am?' The old man replied, 'No, but if you ask one of the nurses over there, she will tell you.'

A classic story is told of a young mother out walking her baby when a friendly stranger stopped her, peered into the pram and exclaimed, 'What a beautiful child!' 'Oh', said the mother, apparently not much flattered, 'you ought to see his photograph.' In these times there are constant efforts to persuade us that the image is more real than the reality.

Homily at AHISA Senior Staff Conference Service, 17 April 2001

God and greatness of heart

Some of you might remember the story of the Air Florida flight that crashed into the icy waters of the Potomac River just after taking off from Washington airport in 1982. There were only six survivors, all in the water clinging to a fragment of the plane's tail section.

Only minutes were available for a rescue before the survivors would freeze to death in the water, so there was no time to send a boat. There was only one small helicopter, which could handle just one person at a time, hovering over the survivors, lowering a lifeline and flotation ring, waiting till the person was holding tight, and then dashing to the shore for safety.

Each time the helicopter returned and lowered its line, one of the survivors, a middle-aged, balding man with a great moustache, would grab hold of the flotation ring, and pass it to one of the others with him in the water. When at last the other five had been rescued and the helicopter returned for him, the man was gone. Overcome by the cold, he had slipped quietly to his death in the dark freezing waters of the Potomac River.

We ask ourselves what could possibly prepare a person to respond so instinctively with such greatness of heart?

Homily, 22 September 2002

God never short changes us

The story is told of the little boy who wrote to Santa Claus with a desperate plea: could Santa please send $500 right away because Mum and him and the other kids need it badly. The letter addressed to Santa arrived at the post office of the small town and was passed on to a local charity known as the Helpers. Without waiting for the next meeting or an organized appeal, several of the members pooled their resources and got a $300 cheque off to the boy. They accompanied the cheque with a little note signed 'Santa's Helpers.

A week later, another letter for Santa arrived at the post office: 'Dear Santa, thank you very much for answering so quickly. That was great! Your friend, Tom. Post Script: Next time could you send it straight to me – those Helpers of yours take a big commission!' (Quoted in Catherine Hammond, *Stories to Hold an Audience*, E. J. Dwyer, Newtown, 1994, p. 118).

Homily, 23 December 2001

We become like God by doing what God does

Quite a few years ago there was a film called The Man Who Played God. The main character was a prominent, rich musician who became bitter, angry and cynical with life because he was losing his hearing. Not only did he turn his back on his friends, he also turned his back on God. He moved into a penthouse where he began to learn the art of lip-reading. From his penthouse window, overlooking a park, he would look through a set of high-powered binoculars and try to read people's lips.

One day he concentrated on a young man whose lips were moving in prayer. He determined what it was the young man was praying for and then dispatched his butler to deliver it to him. On another occasion he read the lips of a woman who was telling another about something she needed and wanted desperately. Again, the wealthy musician saw to it that she received what she needed. And each time he performed one of these services, the cynical musician would look up to heaven and laugh in God's face. He found it laughable that he was playing God but didn't believe in God.

As time went by, however, and he kept reading peoples' lips and fulfilling their needs, a strange thing happened to the rich musician. The man who was playing at being God started to discover God and love him again. Through the game he was playing – the game of serving people's needs – the very God he didn't believe in became real to him, because God is a God of service.

Homily, 26 August 2001.

Christ the King of Hearts

It has been written anonymously that Jesus Christ was 'a young man who was born in an obscure village, the child of a peasant woman … He worked in a carpenter shop until he was thirty. He never wrote a book. He never held an office. He never owned a home. He never had a family. He never went to university … He never did one of the things that usually accompany greatness. He had no credentials but himself.

'While he was still a young man the tide of public opinion turned against him. His friends ran away. He was turned over to his enemies … He was nailed to a cross between two thieves. While he was dying, his executioners gambled for the only piece of property he had on earth, and that was his coat. When he was dead, he was laid in a borrowed grave through the pity of a friend.

'Nineteen, nearly twenty centuries have come and gone, and today he is the leader of the column of progress. I am far within the mark when I say that all the armies that ever marched, and all the kings who ever reigned, put together, have not affected the life of man upon this earth as has that One Solitary Life.'

I think the anonymous writer here gives us the answer to what sort of king Jesus was. He was not a king over land or territory, but he was a King of Hearts. The only power he had was the power of love.

The Feast of Christ the King, King of Hearts, asks us what rules our heart. What motivates us, moves us, what drives us along in life, and how? What and whom do we make time for? The other day I read about the young father who used to love to read to his little daughter every night before she went to sleep. As he became busier and busier in his job, he found this reading time difficult so he bought his little girl a tape recorder and taught her how to use the tape and listen to the stories read on it. One night he came home fairly late and went into his daughter's room and found her crying on her chair. He asked her what was the matter, and she said he never read to her any more. He said he gave her a tape recorder for this purpose. She burst out crying again and said, 'But I can't sit on a tape recorder's knee'. In other words, a tape recorder can't convey a father's love, can't share its heart with another.

Homily, 25 November 2000

Let me draw this reflection to a conclusion by mentioning other images that have drawn me to find God in recent times:

Steve Waugh's wife, after his sacking as the One Day Australian Cricket Captain, said, 'Things happen for a reason. It mightn't be clear right now, but it will work out in the end' (*Daily Telegraph*, 16 February 2002). To say that nothing happens by chance is, for me, to posit a broader plan or scheme of things in God.

Nothing ever happens by chance. When a French artillery man in the battle of Pamplona in 1521 fired a cannon ball that shattered the leg of Ignatius Loyola, he changed his whole life. In changing the whole life of Ignatius, that French artillery man changed our lives too.

All of us have been changed by the Order, the Society of Jesus, the Jesuits, founded by Ignatius. Without that Order, none of us would be at Riverview today – for the simple reason that there would be no Riverview. We are part of a world-wide Jesuit network which contains schools, universities, parishes, all sorts of people working with the poor and marginalized in every country of the world.

Nothing ever happens by chance. Dom John Chapman wrote words with which St Ignatius could resonate easily: 'Every moment is the message of God's will; every external event, everything outside us, and even every involuntary thought and feeling, within us is God's own touch. We are living in God, in God's action, as a fish in water.'

Nothing ever happens by chance. Today we celebrate with great thanksgiving our part in this great Jesuit family of students, staff, parents, friends and old scholars across the world. Nothing ever happens by chance.

St Ignatius' Day Homily, 31 July 2001

'God's a jazz lover and she'll make it good.' So said a woman radio listener, predicting that a jazz festival in Wollstonecraft, Sydney, would go ahead in gloomy, uncertain weather.

The Celtic notion of 'thin places'. The Irish regard some places as especially sacred, as 'thin places', where there is barely a dividing line, just a thin membrane, between the spiritual world and the material world. A 'thin place' connects the seen and unseen worlds and allows the inhabitants of each world to cross over to the other. A 'thin place' for us is a place where it is possible to touch and be touched by God as well as the angels, the saints, and those who have died. Where and when does God permeate the membrane for you?

One can easily find God in the enthusiasm of the people around us, understanding that the word 'enthusiasm' comes from the two Greek words *en* and *theos* meaning 'in God'. Enthusiastic people can lead us to God.

There is a lovely image of God as a potter in the Bible. As I watch a visual arts teacher helping a student to paint, draw or pot, it is easy to think of God caring for and molding creatively each individual.

Not so long ago, I attended a staff seminar on 'Finding God in all things' in which the teachers came up with all sorts of examples from their teaching experience: the making of a clock and consequent reflections on time and eternity in teaching Design and Technology; meeting Christ in the poor at Matthew Talbot Hostel for homeless men; encountering God in the precision and togetherness of rowing; reflecting on hell as a place without God in Studies of Religion class; grappling with chaos theory in Mathematics and the immensity of the universe in Physics; seeing and reflecting on God's presence in the beauty of nature during year level camps and Duke of Edinburgh Award expeditions; discerning God in the characters of *To Kill a Mocking Bird*.

These last examples are very familiar to us all, I am sure. In referring to games and sport, there is a splendid scene in the film *Chariots of Fire*, when the great Scottish sprinter, Eric Liddell, exclaims: 'When I run like the wind, I feel God's pleasure.' Placing principle before expedience, he refused to bow to pressure to run in the qualifying heats on Sundays during the 1924 Paris Olympic Games. Sundays belonged to God for Liddell.

As a keen golfer, I often think that a game of golf is very similar to one's spiritual journey in life. Well-known American author, M. Scott Peck, certainly agrees. He has written an entire book on the topic – *Golf and the Spirit: Lessons for the Journey*. 'Keep your head down' and 'align your hands with your heart' are as important maxims for golf as they are for life, for learning to pray, and finding God in all things.

At the very end of George Bernanos' classic French novel, *Diary of a Country Priest*, which depicts the corruption and excesses of the Church of the day, the good and honest young curate is dying of painful stomach cancer. His friend, who is with him, has sent for the priest to administer the last rites and they are waiting for him to arrive. The friend writes: 'the priest was still on his way, and finally I was bound to voice my deep regret that such a delay threatened to deprive my comrade of the final consolation of the church … He then uttered these words … And I am quite sure that I have recorded them accurately, for his voice, though halting, was strangely distinct: "Does it matter? Grace is everywhere."'

> Lord, help me see the world
> with the same beauty it had
> when it tumbled from your creative hand.
> Help me see that
> nothing here below is profane.
> On the contrary, everything is sacred.

Pierre Teilhard de Chardin sj

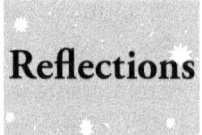

Reflections

Footprints

Last night I had a dream. I dreamed I was walking along the beach with the Lord and across the sky flashed scenes from my life. For each scene I noticed two sets of footprints in the sand; one belonged to me, the other to the Lord.

When the last scene of my life flashed before us I looked back at the footprints in the sand.

I noticed that at many times along the path of life, there was only one set of footprints.

I also noticed that it happened at the very lowest and saddest times of my life. This really bothered me, so I questioned the Lord about it.

'Lord, you said that once I decided to follow you, you would walk with me all the way. But I have noticed that during the most troublesome times in my life, there was only one set of footprints. I don't understand why in times when I needed you most, you would leave me.'

The Lord replied, 'My precious child, I love you and I would never, never leave you during times of trial and suffering. When you see only one set of footprints, it was then that I carried you'.

Author unknown

> 'Yahweh, your God, goes in front of you and will be fighting on your side as you saw him fight for you in Egypt. In the wilderness, too, you saw him: how Yahweh carried you, as a man carries his child, all along the road you travelled on the way to this place.'
> Deuteronomy 1:30-31.

> You take the pen,
> and the lines dance.
> You take the flute,
> and the notes shimmer.
> You take the brush,
> and the colors sing.
> So all things have meaning and beauty
> in that space beyond time where you are.
> How, then, can I hold anything from you?
>
> Dag Hammarskjöld

Nothing Wasted

Lily and I have a beautiful flower garden which we have relished tending over the years. Flower gardens do not just happen. To develop a really fine flower garden takes an enormous amount of money and time and love and care. It would be inconceivable for me to take a bulldozer or a flamethrower and just devastate the garden that we have poured so much energy and care into. That's my feeling about life after death. Knowing God's efficiency, it makes no sense to me that She/He should put so much energy into developing souls just to obliterate them, to waste them. There must be something more.

M. Scott Peck, *Further along the Road Less Travelled*, pp. 172-173.

Busy inside

Prior to gaining notoriety as an outstanding scientist and theologian, Father Pierre Teilhard de Chardin SJ spent some time as a chaplain in the trenches during the First World War.

After four years at the front, he was given the *Croix de Guerre*, the military medal, and the Legion of Honour. While machine guns were still sweeping the ground, he would dash out close to enemy lines, find a wounded man, pick him up on his back, and crawl to the rear. The men in his platoon complained that he did too much. The victims were often dead anyway.

The men frequently saw that he was 'busy inside'. He was indeed, busy with the dazzling Presence running through all creation. 'More than ever I believe life is beautiful, in the grimmest circumstances when you can see God, ever-present, in them' (Letter to Claude Aragonnès, 28 May 1915).

W. J. O'Malley, *The Fifth Week*, p. 103.

> Both what you run away from – and yearn for – is within you
> Behold God beholding you … and smiling
>
> Anthony De Mello SJ

In God's hands

Every night
I turn my worries over to God –
he's going to be up all night anyway.

Mary Crowley

When night comes
and you look
back over the day
and see how fragmentary
everything has been,
and how much you planned
that has gone undone,
and all the reasons
you have been embarrassed and ashamed:
just take everything
exactly as it is, put it
in God's hands
and leave it with Him.
Then you will
be able to rest in Him
– really rest –
and start the next day
as a new life.

Blessed Teresa Benedicta of the Cross OCD
(Edith Stein)

A blessing

… while it's very difficult
For humankind to understand
God's intentions and his purpose
And the workings of his hand,
If we observe the miracles
That happen every day,
We cannot help but be convinced
That in his wondrous way
God makes what seemed unbearable
And painful and distressing
Easily acceptable
When we view it as a blessing.

Virginia J. Ruehlmann, *The Poems and Prayers of Helen Steiner Rice*

In every trouble or problem, there is a blessing. It takes patience and perseverance to see it. Improve my outlook, Lord, so that I can see clearly the blessings you have sent my way.

Cardinal Hume on God and prayer

A man who afterwards became a prominent Christian said that his idea of God was revolutionized when, as a little boy, he was taken to visit an old lady.

The old lady pointed out to him a text on her wall – 'Thou, God, seest me' – and she said to him, 'You see those words. They do not mean God is always watching you to see what you are doing wrong, they mean he loves you so much that he cannot take his eyes off you' …

A very precious way to pray is just through silence. No thoughts or words, just wanting to be silent in the presence of God. Perhaps one of the high points in prayer is where two silences meet: God's silence and our silence. No need for thoughts – and words get in the way.

Cardinal Basil Hume, *In My Own Words*, Hodder & Stoughton, 1999

A Prayer for courage, wisdom, faith and love

Lord, grant us

Courage to do right
when doing wrong or nothing at all
would be easier.

Wisdom to say the right thing at the right time
because words have the power to help or to hurt.

Faith in the goodness of humankind
because living in doubt and fear is not living as you
meant it to be.

And, most important, Love,

The kind that gives without demanding,
supports without holding too tightly,
And understands that we are, all of us, imperfect.

The image of the eagle

The eagle flies over its little ones; without pressing heavily upon them it glides, touching them and not touching them. This image of the eagle hovering above the nest is a beautiful one. The transcendence and majesty of God does not impose, does not smother us, but invites and beckons us to open our hearts and to feed on his love.

I often tell the story of a chapel in Switzerland where I used to go and pray when I was a student, and there were lots of things written on the wall: 'Thank you for saving my life' – and one particular one: 'Thank you for not answering my prayer.' That is very profound. No prayer of asking is ever refused. You don't necessarily get the thing you ask for but you get the thing that draws you closer to God and that's what matters.

Cardinal Basil Hume, *In My Own Words*, Hodder & Stoughton, 1999.

In the hands of God

More than ever I find myself in the hands of God.
This is what I have wanted all my life from my youth.
But now there is a difference;
the initiative is entirely with God.
It is indeed a profound spiritual experience
to know and feel myself so totally in God's hands.

Pedro Arrupe SJ composed this prayer after he suffered a debilitating stroke in 1980, the effects of which he patiently endured for the final ten years of his life.

Memo from God

To: You
Date: Today
From: The Boss
Subject: Yourself
Reference: Life

I am God. I will be handling all of your problems. Please remember that I do not need your help.

If life happens to deliver a situation to you that you cannot handle, do not attempt to resolve it. Kindly put it in the SFGTD (Something for God to do) box. All situations will be resolved, but in my time, not yours.

Once the matter is placed into the box, do not hold onto it by worrying about it. Instead, focus on all the wonderful things that are present in your life now.

If you find yourself stuck in traffic, don't despair. There are people in this world for whom driving is an unheard of privilege.

Should you have a bad day at work, think of the man who has been out of work for years.

Should you despair over a relationship gone bad, think of the person who has never known what it's like to love and be loved in return.

Should you grieve the passing of another weekend, think of the woman in dire straits, working twelve hours a day, seven days a week to feed her children.

Should your car break down, leaving you miles away from assistance, think of the paraplegic who would love the opportunity to take that walk.

Should you notice a new grey hair in the mirror, think of the cancer patient in chemo who wishes she had hair to examine.

Should you find yourself at a loss and pondering what is life all about, asking what is my purpose? be thankful. There are those who didn't live long enough to get the opportunity.

Should you find yourself the victim of other people's bitterness, ignorance, smallness or insecurities, remember, things could be worse. You could be one of them.

Should you decide to send this to a friend, thank you, you may have touched their life in ways you will never know!

Part of us in what we create

Some people say that in the artist's work you will see something of the artist, and for me this is the closest and best analogy. If you look at a work of art you will always see something of the artist. Some people can recognize composers: that is Mozart, for example, or that is Beethoven. We leave part of ourselves in what we create, and that is a simple thought about God: He has left part of himself in His creation. It is through that that we can build up our picture of what God is like.

Cardinal Basil Hume, *In My Own Words*, Hodder & Stoughton, 1999

A Prayer

God, in this world of mixed and changing values,
I ask for myself, for others,
the wisdom to distinguish between the important

and the unimportant, the true and the false,
the trivial and the eternal.

Sometimes I do not know which way to turn.
There are so many claims on my time,
so many demands on my attention.

Life pulls me in so many directions,
and presents me with so many possibilities.
At times I am confused and don't know what to do.

It is then that I need you,
for you are a light for my path
and a lamp in the darkness of my mind.

God, I want to be your faithful disciple,
help me to see what to do.
Give me a listening ear and an open heart
to follow you wherever you want me to go.

Author unknown

A God-seeker

Some excerpts from Jesuit poet Peter Steele's splendid homily at Sister Deirdre Rofe's Requiem Mass at St Patrick's Cathedral, Melbourne, 22 August 2002.

She was above all a God seeker: a tracer of his many signs in her milieu – in her world, in her work, and in her relationships. One of the things which made her so deeply attractive was her evident sense that there was more to common events and circumstances than their ordinary face: and that 'more' was good, and promising, and fertile. She spoke and acted, and indeed she looked, as if life was a sponsored thing, and as if each day was a sponsored day …

And she also knew that what she was being sponsored into was God-seeking, God-questing, whether it was in the suppressed groans of a Monday, or the 'Thank-God' of a Friday. She knew that in the end the calendar is a kind of joke, and the enduring cycles of God's movements turn, instead, perpetually in the heart.

Another great poet, John Keats, who like Deirdre died earlier than we could wish, wrote in a letter to someone, that he 'has a purpose, and his eyes are bright with it'. Those who know and loved Deirdre, and who love her still, will agree I think that she too was 'bright-eyed with purpose'. As often as not, she was smiling the while – which does not alter the fact that her purpose was the discovery of divine action in just this world, and the disclosure of that action …

Deirdre quite certainly believed that we are courted by God: and she had good reason for her belief. It answered to Christianity's own testimony, and it answered to her own experience. Socially, she was charm itself: administratively, she could give lessons to most experts: intellectually, she moved in company as dolphins move in the water.

And all the time, as it was and is my pleasure to read her, this kind of miming of what was being done in her by that spirited one whom we call the 'Holy Spirit'. Whenever she starred, as often she did, the gleaming of God was showing through.

Clinging to God

Malcolm Muggeridge wrote: 'It has been said that when human beings stop believing in God they believe in nothing. The truth is even worse: they believe in anything.' Cling to God whatever the corruption of the state, the authoritarianism of the church, the fragility of the family, the perfidy of friends. In all those losses, one truth remains on which we can rely: God is. And that truth remains.

Joan Chittister, *Songs of Joy*, p. 79.

God speaks

New billboards were getting some attention in Arizona during 2002 (and previously Ohio). Some reported seeing one or two messages, but the newspaper listed all of them. Here's a list of all variations of the 'God Speaks' billboards. The billboards are a simple black background with white text. No fine print or sponsoring organization is included.

Tell the kids I love them. — God

Let's meet at my house Sunday before the game. — God

C'mon over and bring the kids. — God

What part of 'thou shall not …' didn't you understand — God

We need to talk. — God

Keep using my name in vain, and I will make rush hour longer. — God

Loved the wedding, invite me to the marriage. — God

That 'Love Thy Neighbor' thing … I meant it. — God

I love you and you and you and you … — God

Will the road you're on get you to my place? — God

Follow me. — God

Big Bang Theory, you've got to be kidding. — God

My way is the highway. — God

Need directions? — God

You think it's hot here? — God

Do you have any idea where you're going? — God

Don't make me come down there. — God

Explaining God

One of God's main jobs is making people. He makes them to replace the ones that die so there will be enough people to take care of things on earth. He doesn't make grown-ups, just babies. I think because they are smaller and easier to make. That way, he doesn't have to take up his valuable time teaching them to talk and walk. He can just leave that to mothers and fathers.

God's second most important job is listening to prayers. An awful lot of this goes on, since some people, like priests and things, pray all the time, not just at bedtime.

God sees everything and hears everything and is everywhere, which keeps him pretty busy. So you shouldn't go wasting his time by going over your mum's and dad's heads and asking for something they say you couldn't have.

Jesus is God's son. He used to do all the hard work like walking on water and performing miracles and trying to teach the people who didn't want to learn about God. They finally got tired of him preaching to them and they crucified him. But he was good and kind like his father and he told his father that they didn't know what they were doing, to forgive them, and God said OK.

His dad (God) appreciated everything he had done and all his hard work on earth so he told him he didn't have to go out on the road any more. He could stay in heaven – so he did.

And now he helps his dad out by listening to prayers and seeing things which are important for God to take care of and which ones he can take care of himself without having to bother God. Like a secretary, only more important. You can pray any time you want and they're sure to hear you because they have got it worked out so one of them is on duty all the time.

If you don't believe in God, besides being an atheist you will be very lonely, because your parents can't go everywhere with you, but God can. It is good to know he's around you when you're scared in the dark or when you can't swim very good and you get thrown in to real deep water by big kids. But you shouldn't just always think of what God can do for you. I figure God put me here and he can take me back any time he pleases. And that's why I believe in God.

Danny Dutton, age 8

Star eight

Living on the move

> *I only wish that [William] Blake had lived long enough to hear quantum physicists speaking like poets, Alan Sandage, for example, confirming that 'every atom in our bodies was once inside a star'.*
> **Kathleen Norris, *Amazing Grace***

Breakfast in the Jesuit community has often been the occasion for successful negotiation of some business for the day ahead. 'Can you fill in for me here?' 'Will you help me out there?' On our Founder's feast day in July 2000, I was wondering aloud what theme I might take for my homily at the School Mass, when our resident guru, Gerald Coleman, looked up from his newspaper and gave me the lead I needed.

Gerald asked me, in his characteristically provocative way, whether I had noticed the one word written at the bottom of the beautiful Tom Bass bronze statue of St Ignatius on the wall outside the Ramsay Hall. To my shame, despite having driven and walked past it countless times, I had never noticed the word 'pilgrim' there. Indeed, Ignatius looked on himself, signed himself, and spoke fondly of himself as 'the pilgrim'.

In the late nineteenth century, a tourist from the United States paid a visit to a famous Polish Rabbi, Hofetz Chaim. He was astonished to see that the Rabbi's dwelling was just a simple room with a desk and a chair. 'Rabbi', asked the tourist, 'where is your furniture?' 'Where is yours?' replied the Rabbi. 'Mine?' asked the puzzled American. 'But I am only a visitor here. I'm only passing through.' To which the Rabbi responded, 'Aren't we all?'

All of us, of course, are pilgrims in this life. We are just passing through. It is the same message conveyed by that one word 'Eternity' illuminated on the Sydney Harbour Bridge for the New Year millennium celebrations and beamed to millions of television viewers across the world. Of what value is it for us to achieve success in this short life if we have lost focus on the real purpose of life, 'eternity'?

If we are to travel though life with the spirit of a true pilgrim, we need to travel light. One cannot carry too much baggage. Those of us who do carry additional inner luggage like resentments, fears, prejudices and failures to forgive, will not move very far in life at all. The way we travel is just as important, if not more important, than arriving at a destination. That is why novelist Robert Louis Stevenson could write, 'To travel hopefully is a better thing than to arrive, and the true success is to labour.'

The remarkable priest and prolific author, Henri Nouwen, wrote that we make two journeys in life – the outer journey as citizens of the world, and the inner journey into freedom, the freedom of spirit born of stillness and self-awareness.

Such an inner journey is at the heart of our spirituality. To be aware of our inner life as a complex mixture of memories, thoughts, emotions, desires and fears is to understand how it affects the way we perceive the world, act in it and react to it. The inner journey is a journey into self-awareness. This quality of soul, which we would like to see nurtured in all our students, is crucial if they are to make sense of an increasingly complex world.

Echoing these sentiments and reflecting on another great journey – that made by the Israelites to escape slavery in Egypt, through

Living on the move — 157

the wilderness and into the land where they could achieve their full promise – Professor Hedley Beare gave this advice in 1982 to a group of graduating students at St Leonard's College in Brighton, Victoria. It will remain fresh and relevant for graduates every year:

> Note these four things about that journey:
> First, you live in a tent. Not in a permanent dwelling, symbolically speaking.
> You must always be on the move – intellectually, metaphorically, spiritually.
> You are a pilgrim, searching for the land in which you will become what you know you want to be.
> The land you move through is a wilderness, never fully comprehended, and always somewhat wild and untamed. Accept the fact that we all are tracking through unknown land.
> Inside your tent, you can keep very little that has lasting meaning. A few rules to guide your behavior, an altar to which you bring your hopes and dreams, and very little else. You can't afford to become attached to mere things and ideas and stay on the move.
> But always remember that the tent, the tabernacle, was invented to remind us about a pillar of cloud by day, and a pillar of fire by night, which accompanies us on our journeying.

In this context of graduates and their journeying, I was much moved by a letter from one pilgrim of the Riverview Class of 1998. He had deferred his studies to work with the poorest of the poor in Calcutta, and this excerpt describes life with them on Howrah railway station:

> I do not want to paint a picture of this work being all doom and gloom. There have been triumphant images that I'll never forget, such as a leper, fingers gnawed away from disease, walking up to me at snail's pace, concentrating so as not to spill the cup of tea, wedged between his stumpy hands, which he offered me as thanks

for changing his bandages. Today, a stinking hot summer day, a man with a leprous ankle bought me a bottle of soft drink as he was concerned for me in the heat.

It is touching that in all their financial despair that these people would still treat volunteers, who could well be dismissed as cashed-up foreigners, with so much respect and generosity. This sense of community, whether it be sharing food or allowing us, as outsiders, to become insiders, is perhaps the most important thing to the families of Howrah station.

The great Cardinal John Henry Newman said once that 'to grow is to change, and to become perfect is to have changed many times.' It seems that we must constantly say farewell to various stages of our life, if we are to move on to a new stage of growth.

Given the importance of 'attitude' in this book, we could not give any credence to Phillip Adams' typically acerbic comment that adolescence is 'a brief period of optimism separating a brief period of ignorance from a terminal period of cynicism.' Rather, we would resonate much more clearly with the hopeful sentiments of Melbourne poet, Chris Wallace-Crabbe, in his lovely poem, 'A Threshold for My Son':[1]

> You touch the door now, trembling on its hinge
> between vague adolescence and the dark
> exciting world an adult stumbles in.
> (Those are not monsters: they are only gum trees,
> so take it easy.) You are seventeen
>
> and nothing is mysterious about that,
> except that all maturing somehow is
> a journey through an unmapped, shadowy park:
> black trees, bird-cries, lugubrious pond
> but nothing you can firmly recognize.

---

[1] Chris Wallace-Crabbe, 'A Threshold for My Son', from *Whirling*, Carcanet Oxford Poets, Oxford University Press, 1998.

> You do not know what teams you're going to play,
> nor even what the local rules may be,
> but play you must, at times heroically
> and yet on other days just getting by:
> having enough of the ball to earn your place.
>
> Today I spied an eagle floating slowly
> along the ridge, taking a bird's-eye-view
> of luck below; it hung at ease
> on the blue air, and yet was governed by
> a fine-tuned observation of the world;
>
> that's the balance to be striven for,
> a cool, difficult strategy, defining life
> at the high, blue behest of happiness.
> Walk tall, dear son.
> Go straight ahead in joy
> making the grassy landscape all your own.

It is a sometimes painful fact of life that, unless we leave one place and stage of life, we cannot begin in another. In another poem, 'Walking Away',[2] Cecil Day-Lewis captures this very well when he says:

> It is eighteen years ago, almost to the day –
> A sunny day with leaves just turning,
> The touch-lines new-ruled – since I watched you play
> Your first game of football, then, like a satellite
> Wrenched from its orbit, go drifting away
>
> Behind a scatter of boys, I can see
> You walking away from me towards the school
> With the pathos of a half-fledged thing set free
> Into a wilderness, the gait of one
> Who finds no path where the path should be.

---

[2] C. Day-Lewis, 'Walking Away', in John Wain (ed), *Anthology of Contemporary Poetry*, Hutchison & Co, London, 1979. See also Jill Balcon (ed), *The Complete Poems*, Sinclair-Stevenson, 1992.

> That hesitant figure, eddying away
> Like a winged seed loosened from its parent stem,
> Has something I never quite grasp to convey
> About nature's give-and-take – the small, the scorching
> Ordeals which fire one's irresolute clay.
>
> I have had worse partings, but none that so
> Gnaws at my mind still. Perhaps it is roughly
> Saying what God alone could perfectly show –
> How selfhood begins with a walking away,
> And love is proved in the letting go.

In this context of saying 'good bye' and moving on, I have often referred to a letter – mentioned already in the book (see p. 71) – from a French parent giving his expectations of a Jesuit school:

> One arrives at a fresh stage of life only by freeing oneself from the last; by a renunciation. The process of growth is a series of renunciations: renunciation of womb-life, of breast-feeding, of exclusive love of the mother; renunciation of the cushioned atmosphere of home in favour of the brisker one of school; renunciation of the self-satisfied comfort of intellectual sufficiency in favour of the adventurous one of the spirit. There can be no checks, no resting-places. Stop at any stage of the journey and you will find that you settle down, you make yourself a refuge.

Among the great early Jesuits, Father Jerome Nadal had the reputation of being someone who clearly understood and luminously articulated the vision of Ignatius the Pilgrim. He wrote: 'The ultimate and even the most preferable of the Society's dwellings are not the professed houses but the highways ... We identify the Society's finest and ultimate dwelling of the professed fathers with a journey'. Many years later, Gerard Hughes, in his marvellous book *In Search of a Way*,[3] reflected that 'we totter and

---

[3] Gerard W. Hughes, *In Search of a Way: Two Journeys of Spiritual Discovery*, DLT, London, 2000, pp. 126-127.

stagger in our search and take wrong routes, but that is better than sitting still'. Ignatius' spirit of searching 'characterized the early Jesuits who travelled all over the world and were so inventive and imaginative.' Sadly, 'when they became well-known and established they reflected the transformation from a pilgrim Church to a parade-ground Church'.

At the end of January 1994, the Governor-General of the time, Bill Hayden, used his Australia Day address to reflect on the recent return of the Unknown Soldier's remains to the Australian War Memorial in Canberra. He remarked:

> To put it simply, I found it a deeply spiritual experience. And by that I mean something that reaches into the far corners of one's psyche, that floods the soul with transcending sentiments about values far greater than the self or one's daily concerns. It was best summed up by the old digger, Mr. Robert Comb, when he sprinkled soil from the Western Front on the coffin and said, 'You're home mate.'[4]

'You're home mate.' The Governor-General went on to say that being 'at home' is much more than a physical presence. It is a 'commitment to the core values of what it means to be an Australian', 'those enduring principles that have made this country what it is ...', a country that, 'for all the great changes that have taken place over 75 years, the Unknown Australian Soldier would still recognize in its essentials, that he would know as home ... Decency. Justice. Tolerance. Comradeship. A sense of common national purpose'. Such are the 'values far greater than the self or one's daily concerns.'

It is a strange paradox in life that, while we must always live on the move, we must also be at home to ourselves and know where our true home is located if we are to grow in humanity. Like the

---

[4] Australia Day Message by the Governor-General of the Commonwealth of Australia, The Honorable Bill Hayden, 26 January 1994, p. 2.

homing pigeon we too need a homing instinct which enables us to be at home with ourselves, at home with our God, and at home with people of all persuasions. None has captured this so succinctly and so beautifully as St Augustine: 'Lord, our hearts are restless until they rest in Thee.'

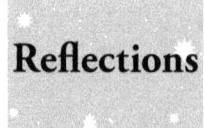

Reflections

Life is a journey

Birth is a beginning
And death a destination
And life is a journey:
From childhood to maturity and youth to age;
From innocence to awareness, from ignorance to knowing;
From foolishness to discretion and then,
Perhaps, to wisdom;
From weakness to strength
Or strength to weakness and, often, back again;
From health to sickness, and back, we pray,
To health again;
From offence to forgiveness, from loneliness to love,
From joy to gratitude, from pain to compassion;
From grief to understanding, from fear to faith;
From defeat to defeat to defeat …
Until, looking backward or ahead,
We see that victory lies
Not at some high place along the way,
But in having made the journey, stage by stage.

Old Hebrew Prayer

Bless the road

And heaven hold and watch your way forever
May your every dream come true
Forgive all wrong, always be strong
And do what you must do
You stand before this open door
And you must now go through
My precious friend, my own my sweet companion
Bless the road that carries you
My precious friend, my own my sweet companion
Bless the road that carries you.
The final verse from the song, 'Bless the Road',
from Irish singer Mary Black's beautiful CD

The Journey

A century from now, what shall be said of our journey in these times?
And who shall the shapers have been? ...
The hopeful dreamers who were strong enough to suffer for the dream?
Or the fearful pessimists who were convinced that dreaming and hope are for sleepers only, not for those awake to the age?
A century from now, shall hope and humour have been strong enough to enable living with unanswerable questions?
Or shall the pain that a transitional age necessarily brings have caused a retreat to old answers
that no longer acknowledge new questions?
A century from now, we shall have journeyed ... backward or forward.
Direction can no longer be given by circumstance;
real journeyers know that the direction is always chosen by

those who make the journey. Who shall choose the direction?
... So the question is still the same ...
A century from now, what shall be said of our human journey in these times?
And who shall the shapers have been?
Lillian Smith, 'The Journey', 1954

Letting go

Your children are not your children.
They are the sons and daughters of Life's longing for itself.
They come through you but not from you,
And though they are with you yet they belong not to you ...

You are the bows from which your children
as living arrows are sent forth.
The archer sees the mark upon the path of the infinite,
and He bends you with His might
that His arrows may go swift and far.
Let your bending in the archer's hand be for gladness;
For even as He loves the arrow that flies,
so He loves also the bow that is stable.
Kahlil Gibran, *The Prophet*

Transitions in life

The growing-up process provides many examples of how we have to die in order to reach the next stage of living. The child in us has to die before we become an independent teenager, and we do not become such until we have put away the cosy privileges and protectedness of the child.

There is, incidentally, a parallel transition going on in the life of the parents who have to put away the protective attitudes appropriate to parents of a child and learn the new, more trusting activities appropriate to parents of adolescents. In few cases is the transition smooth and untroubled, so it is comforting to notice that Joseph and Mary also had a small crisis on their hands when Jesus began to show the independence of a teenager (Luke 2:41-51).

Jock Dalrymple, 'Dying before Death', *The Ampleforth Journal*

Saying goodbye

Another area of life where we successively die to be reborn is that of parting. How poignant parting is; how difficult it is! Personally, I never get used to parting, either from places or from people. Am I alone in having found that it is just as sad to leave a place where I have been unhappy as it is to leave a place where I have been happy? In both cases, the places where I have lived and worked, the house, the streets, the landscape, twine themselves round my heart like ivy round a tree-trunk. Every corner has a memory which tugs at me to keep me from leaving. *Partir – c'est mourir un peu.* It really is. Leaving people is, of course, even more difficult than leaving places. I do not think John Henry Newman at all overdid the poignancy in his sermon at Littlemore, 'The Parting of Friends', in 1843. It is every bit as sad as he said:

> And, O my brethren, O kind and affectionate hearts, O loving friends, should you know anyone whose lot it has been, by writing or by word of mouth, in some degree to help you thus to act; if he has ever told you what you knew about yourselves, or what you did not know; has read to you your wants and feelings, and comforted you by the very reading; has made you feel that there was a higher life than this daily one, and a brighter world than that you can see; or encouraged you, or sobered you, or opened a way to the inquiring, or soothed the perplexed; if what he has said or done has ever made you take interest in him, and feel well inclined towards him; remember such a one ...'

And yet we know that unless we part from one place and stage in life we cannot begin another. Our affection for the first has to be released and purified before we can treat the new place with seriousness and respect. So also with colleagues and friends.

Jock Dalrymple, 'Dying before Death', *The Ampleforth Journal*, c. 1982

Focusing the mind and heart

Doctor Johnson wrote once, 'When a man knows he is to be hanged in a fortnight, it concentrates his mind wonderfully.' There is little like the words of Ash Wednesday to focus our minds and hearts on what is really important in life: 'Remember, thou art dust and unto dust thou shalt return.'

'Dust to dust' is not the whole story, of course, because we Christians believe in the resurrection of the body. Nonetheless, it is a healthy reminder to keep life in proper perspective when we find ourselves preoccupied with non-essentials like our looks, health, success, wealth and status.

Remembering that we originate from dust and are dust-destined should free us from much useless anxiety and give us space to see the humorous side of ourselves and of others.

Life, therefore, is a brief interlude between states of dust. The season of Lent brings us back to basics with a thud. Life in the body is a stage on our journey.

'Viewpoint', 2 March 2001

God the centre

Last weekend I was attending a Jesuit Heads of Ministry meeting in Melbourne and at one of our prayer sessions we were introduced to the ancient spiritual idea of the labyrinth. It has become the focus of much spiritual writing recently, but I think it offers us a good metaphor for understanding life's many twists and turns – the journey that all of us are involved in every day and in which your sons are about to begin a new chapter when leaving school in a few months time.

The labyrinth looks like a maze, but unlike a maze it has no dead-ends, barriers or tricks. The single path leads each walker into the labyrinth centre, and the same path leads each pilgrim back out into the world. By keeping an eye on the centre of the labyrinth we can find our way in and out of the maze of interconnecting paths and patterns. It is geography for our inner journey that is paramount here ...

So your young men are about to enter life's labyrinth. How do they find their way to the centre, which is God?

Well, it won't be a straight path, of course. There will be the usual scepticism and cynicism – like that of Nathaniel in the gospel: 'From Nazareth? Can anything good come from that place?' I am sure you have heard that sort of response before. But the simple invitation, 'Come and see', is the only response to that sort of doubt. Come and see for yourself, experience life and find God the centre for yourself.

To find one's way through the labyrinth of life to the Centre, who is God, we need a compass, a direction finder.

We have none better than the love of our Mothers, the knowledge of their fidelity to us, their always being there for us, their love without strings or corners for us. This is our inner map, our inner compass – the love of our mothers – that will help us find our way to the Centre, God.

Our prayer for our boys this morning might be those wonderful words of Paul to the Philippians. We pray that their journey, with all its ups and downs, twists and turns, will be joyful. We pray that they will always sense that the Lord is near to them, that the peace of God who is beyond our understanding will guard their hearts and thoughts in Jesus Christ.

Homily at Year 12 Mothers' Mass, prior to their sons' graduation, 24 August 2001.

A Valete blessing for Graduates

With more than a little help from John O'Donohue and the Irish Blessing.

> May the stars always remind you that you have friends,
> that, however apart, you are together.
>
> May you remember that on the blackest nights
> the stars are at their brightest.
>
> May you recall always with gratitude that you are blessed with
> the best of friends – your family
>
> May you treasure always the friends you have made at school
>
> And remember that friendship is a gift to be treasured, not
> squandered.
>
> May you be good to them and may you be there for them;
> may they bring you all the blessings, challenges, truth and
> light that you need for your journey.
>
> May you learn to be a good friend to your self.
>
> May you be able to journey to that place in your soul where
> there is great love, warmth, feeling and forgiveness.
>
> May this continue to change you.
>
> May you never forget that,
>
> Wherever you journey in life,
>
> Whether you advert it to or not,
>
> You are most richly blessed with the friendship of God.
>
> May the road rise to meet you,
> May the wind be always at your back,
> May the sun shine warm upon your face,
> The rain fall gently in your fields,
> And, until we meet again,
> May God hold you in the hollow of his hands,
> Father, Son, and Holy Spirit.
>
> Amen.

Part 2

Four Canopies*

*Aligned with the
four 'weeks' or segments
of the *Spiritual Exercises* of
St Ignatius of Loyola

Introduction

In the first Introduction to this book, found back on page 3, I recount the lovely story told in a letter home by one of my Year 9 boarding students of 1999. His name is Ed, and I recently had the honour of celebrating the sacrament of marriage with him and his wife Michelle in Bangalore, NSW. The homily I gave at that ceremony reflected on the two readings Ed and Michelle had chosen to mark the occasion. The homily went this way:

To love another is to see the face of God

The readings Ed and Michelle have chosen for us today are beautiful ones – very appropriately, for this is a sacred event in a sacred place at St Kevin's Church, Bangalow.

I happen to love the first reading, from Isaiah chapter 43, especially the words, 'I have called you by your name: you are mine' (43:1). If Michelle can pardon the spotlight being on Ed for the moment, I am very much reminded of the time at Riverview when Ed was a Year 9 boarder and had written home to his parents in Albury in 1999. When his parents Tony and Maree sent me a copy of his letter, I was much moved. Indeed, while its grammar and spelling left a little to be desired, it served as something of the inspiration for the title of a little book of reflections I wrote about four years later. Against the background of the recent death of a family friend ('Bucko', a much loved old boy of the school and father of 'Charlie'), Ed wrote to his parents from his uninterrupted and well-publicised dormitory view of the heavens:

> Every night I gaze up and see three stars I have named the star (one) witch is called mum, star (two) witch is called dad, and star three witch I called (bucko) because of charlies sake and for bucko to help me through school in the hard times because he came here. But I am also looking for two more stars witch I will call poppy/courage and the other will be called pa/hope. I gave them these names because poppy was courageous because he went to war and I called pa/hope because he was farmer who had hope that rain would come in the future to help him. These are my five stars.

What struck me about these beautiful words, of course, was that they seemed very closely aligned to the other source of inspiration for my book – the writing of St Ignatius of Loyola, the founder of the Society of Jesus, who loved to look up in wonder at the star-studded Roman sky at night and contemplate the grandeur of the Creator and his creation. Like Ed, the young student author, Ignatius would name the stars after his Jesuit companions and friends spread out across the globe. What strong companionship and love there is in Andrew Bullen's beautiful words in his poem *Ignatius and the Stars* – 'However apart, we are together!'

Very clearly now Ed has added a new, sixth, star to his vision of the world – obviously his first star is Michelle.

Our second reading is a beautiful Buddhist blessing for the journey, which all of us take every day – a journey from God to God. In early December three years ago, when returning from Auckland, I stopped at the Tullamarine airport's duty-free shop to purchase some spiritual sustenance for my Xavier Jesuit community. After discerning what spirit was most appropriate for my abstemious brethren, I went to the counter to pay for it. The young lady in attendance there greeted me with the question: 'Are you in transition, sir?' 'Yes,' was my reply, 'aren't we all?'

Ed and Michelle are making one of the most wonderful transitions today – from uncommitted people to committed people. One of my favourite writers is a man named Jonathan Sacks, the Chief Rabbi of the Commonwealth. When he was launching National Marriage Week some years ago in England, a pushy interviewer said to him: 'Isn't that very politically incorrect? Who really believes in marriage any more?' To which the good Rabbi responded: 'I do, because in this buy it, use it and throw it away society of ours is there anything more lasting or more gracious than the commitment to share your life with the person you love, and, through that commitment, to bring new life into the world?'

He went on to say: 'Marriage, sanctified by the bond of fidelity, is the nearest life gets to a work of art. It's what I call the poetry of the everyday. And though the moral fashions of today, like yesterday's papers, will one day crumble into dust, of this I am sure: marriage will still be there as the greatest redemption of our loneliness, the point where soul meets soul and we know we are not alone.'

Finally, we come to that wonderful gospel reading from St John where we are challenged to achieve the seemingly impossible – namely, to love one another as God loves us. I read the other day someone saying that there are only three entities that love like God – our mothers, our grandmothers and our pet dogs. All of these love us without any conditions, any strings, any corners, any ties attached. They forgive us no matter what atrocities we have committed. They accept us and love us unconditionally, no matter what. And this is what God does and this is what true love is about. What a challenge!

Several years ago I heard the pastor of the Wayside Chapel in Sydney, the Reverend Graham Long, talking during a radio interview in Brisbane about the hundreds of people who come off the streets and into the Wayside Chapel each day. He said his challenge was to see the beauty in every face, even when the owner of that face had long given up on it. Surely, that is to love others as Jesus did, Jesus the One who never gives up on us.

How on earth are we going to achieve that degree of love – a love without any conditions, any ties, any corners, any strings attached – just pure giving, even to the extent of giving his life for us? The answer is – only with God's help, God's grace, of course. To love another person is a decision, a choice, a commitment we make. As it is said so beautifully in the musical *Les Misérables* , 'to love another person is to see the face of God.' Learning to love another wholeheartedly keeps us close to the heart of God.

So Ed and Michelle have extended some wonderful challenges to all of us today – as well as to themselves. Our prayer for them might be the words quoted by King George VI, in his Christmas Broadcast of 1939 and further made famous in the film *The King's Speech*:

> And I said to the man
> Who stood at the gate of the year,
> 'Give me a light that I may tread safely into the unknown.'
> And he replied.
> 'Go out into the darkness and put your hand into the Hand
>   of God.
> That shall be to you better than a light and safer than
>   a known way!'
>   Minnie Louise Haskins, 'God Knows'

A fire that starts other fires

The underlying platform for my own ongoing Ignatian formation and which I propose for others is described in the following words of Richard Rohr OFM:

> You lead others to the depth to which you have been led ...
> You can only transform people to the degree you have been transformed. You can only lead others as far as you yourself have gone.[1]

---

[1] Richard Rohr, *Things Hidden*, 2008, pp. 43-44

When Ignatius was compiling the *Spiritual Exercises* at Manresa, he often spoke of God dealing with him 'in the same way a school teacher deals with a child, instructing him'. Indeed, he left instructions in the *Spiritual Exercises* that the one 'who is giving the *Exercises* should leave the creator to act immediately with the creature, and the creature with its creator and Lord.' This immediacy of God's interaction with the individual is an essential component of Ignatian spirituality.

In Annotation 7 of the *Spiritual Exercises*, Ignatius requires the retreat director to deal with the retreatant gently and kindly. Again, in Annotation 15, he advises that the one 'who is giving the *Exercises* should not turn or incline to one side or the other, but, standing in the centre like a balance, leave the Creator to act immediately with the creature, and the creature with its Creator and Lord.' These are the roots of what we know as *cura personalis* – care for the individual.

In what we do in the world there must always be a transparency to God. Our lives must provoke the questions, 'who are you, that you do these things … and that you do them in this way?' … Our deep love of God and our passion for his world should set us on fire – a fire that starts other fires!' (Society of Jesus, General Congregation 35, Decree 2, par. 10, 2008).

Canopy one

Ensuring proper perspective and balance in my life

'Trafficking in intangibles ...'
Kathleen Norris

Everything is sacred

For those of us endeavouring constantly to seek and find God in all things, the prayer of that great Jesuit and cosmic adventurer, Teilhard de Chardin, is very appropriate:

> Lord, help me see the world
> with the same beauty it had
> when it tumbled from your
> creative hand.
> Help me see that nothing here below is profane.
> On the contrary, everything is sacred.

adapted from Pierre Teilhard de Chardin, *The Divine Milieu*, 1960*

We praise God not to celebrate our own faith but to give thanks for the faith God has in us. To let ourselves look at God, and let God look back at us. And to laugh, and sing, and be delighted because God has called us his own.
Kathleen Norris, *Amazing Grace*, p. 151

Behold God beholding you ... and smiling.
Tony de Mello sj, from *Hearts on Fire*, Michael Harter sj (ed.), 1993, p. 9

---

* Please see the References, pp. 218–220, for full details for the works cited throughout this section.

Religion and God

In Joan Chittister's wonderful book, *Called to Question*, she relates the following story of some disciples who were distraught at the imminent death of their Master:

'If you leave us, Master', they pleaded, 'how will we know what to do?' And the Master replied, 'I am nothing but a finger pointing at the moon. Perhaps when I am gone you will see the moon.' The meaning is clear: It is God that religion must be about, not itself. When religion makes itself God, it ceases to be religion.

Joan Chittister, *Called to Question*, 2004

All is on loan

There is an ancient Aztec Indian prayer that reflects the preciousness of life and the fleetingness of it:

> Oh, only for so short a while you
> have loaned us to each other,
> because we take form in your act
> of drawing us,
> and we take life in your painting us,
> and we breathe in your singing us.
> But only for so short a while
> have you loaned us to each other.

This 'on loan' philosophy is the first and most important attitude of a pilgrim heart … When we look upon all life as being on loan to us, we look at it differently. We look at this loan for what it is – purely gift, given to us out of love. We reverence all that we have and take great joy in it, but we do not grasp, cling to, or hoard our treasures …

To let go does not mean that we give up or that we do not care. Rather, it means that we choose to use our energies in another way, giving them another direction ... To let go is to allow something or someone to be left behind in such a way that we are free to continue toward new country that is waiting to be revealed to us ... Letting go is an attitude that grows within us. It is never complete until it is acted upon.
Joyce Rupp, *Praying Our Goodbyes*, 1988, pp. 69, 100-101

Everything has a meaning, nothing a price

For someone whose job so obviously mirrors man's extraordinary possibilities and responsibilities, there is no excuse if he loses his sense of 'having been called'. So long as he keeps that, everything he can do has a meaning, nothing a price. Therefore, if he complains, he is accusing – himself.
Dag Hammarskjöld, *Markings* (23/6/57), 1964

If God made us, if God put deep desires into our hearts, isn't the first task of responding to God's will simply to recognize our own deepest desires and to act upon them? I spent so many years in seminary trying to figure out what God wanted, but there was never a day I didn't want to be a teacher. Isn't God clever, hiding the divine will in the last place I would look, my heart?
Terrance W. Klein, *Vanity Faith: Searching for Spirituality among the Stars*, Liturgical Press, 2009, p. 3

Let us be sure that T. S. Eliot's profoundly sad line in *Four Quartets* does not describe our own life: 'We had the experience, but missed the meaning.'

Salvation through love

The following is a famous excerpt from *Man's Search For Meaning* by Viktor Frankl. He was an Austrian Jew, a psychiatrist, and a holocaust survivor. He is writing here about his experience early one morning on the way to a work detail in the infamous Auschwitz camp.

We stumbled on in the darkness, over big stones and through large puddles, along the one road leading from the camp. The accompanying guards kept shouting at us and driving us with the butts of their rifles. Anyone with very sore feet supported himself on his neighbour's arm. Hardly a word was spoken; the icy wind did not encourage talk. Hiding his mouth behind his upturned collar, the man marching next to me whispered suddenly: 'If our wives could see us now! I do hope they are better off in their camps and don't know what is happening to us.'

That brought thoughts of my own wife to mind. And as we stumbled on for miles, slipping on icy spots, supporting each other time and again, dragging one another up and onward, nothing was said, but we both knew: each of us was thinking of his wife. Occasionally I looked at the sky, where the stars were fading and the pink light of the morning was beginning to spread behind a dark bank of clouds. But my mind clung to my wife's image, imagining it with an uncanny acuteness. I heard her answering me, saw her smile, her frank and encouraging look. Real or not, her look was then more luminous than the sun which was beginning to rise.

A thought transfixed me: for the first time in my life I saw the truth as it is set into song by so many poets, proclaimed as the final wisdom by so many thinkers. The truth – that love is the ultimate and the highest goal to which man can aspire. Then I grasped the meaning of the greatest secret that human poetry and human thought and belief have to impart: **The salvation of man is through love and in love.***

---

*Emphasis added.

I did not know whether my wife was alive, and I had no means of finding out (during all my prison life there was no outgoing or incoming mail); but at that moment it ceased to matter. There was no need for me to know; nothing could touch the strength of my love, my thoughts, and the image of my beloved. Had I known then that my wife was dead, I think that I would still have given myself, undisturbed by that knowledge, to the contemplation of her image, and that my mental conversation with her would have been just as vivid and just as satisfying. 'Set me like a seal upon thy heart, love is as strong as death.'

Viktor Frankl, *Man's Search for Meaning*, 1959

How do I love?

How do I love thee? Let me count the ways.
I love thee to the depth and breadth and height
My soul can reach, when feeling out of sight
For the ends of Being and ideal Grace.
I love thee to the level of every day's
Most quiet need, by sun and candlelight.
I love thee freely, as men strive for Right;
I love thee purely, as they turn from Praise.
I love thee with the passion put to use
In my old griefs, and with my childhood's faith.
I love thee with a love I seemed to lose
With my lost saints. I love thee with the breath,
Smiles, tears, of all my life! – and, if God choose,
I shall but love thee better after death.

Elizabeth Barrett Browning, Sonnet XLIII

Searching for God

Some years ago there appeared a very engaging book by Vincent Donovan, a Mill Hill missionary in Africa, called *Christianity Rediscovered* (SCM, 2001). The writer went and lived with the Masai tribe. In one village, he came across a young man who had been searching for God.

This young man had left his tribe, armed with his spear and shield, to track God down. In the area there was a volcano, and the young man felt that if God was to be found anywhere, he was to be found in the midst of the fire and smoke that came from the mountain. But he found nothing, and came back to his tribe disappointed, disenchanted.

The missionary listened to the young man's story, and then said to him,

'You have tried as hard as a man can try. You left your father and family and home and went in search of God up that terrible mountain. You tracked and followed him to his lair, like a lion tracks a wildebeest. But all the time God was tracking you. You did not send for me or look me up. I was sent to you. You thought you were searching for God. All the time he has been searching for you.

'God is more beautiful and loving than you imagined. He hungered for you. Try as we might, we cannot reach up by brute force and drag God down from the heavens. He is already here. He has found you. In truth, we are not the lion looking for God. God is the lion looking for us. Believe me, the lion is God' …

The best starting point for anything we say about the life of faith is to remind ourselves of God the Father's all-embracing and unconditional love for us. He has made us out of love, and he wants us to enjoy love. His other name is Love: we can't get anywhere unless we let that sink into our bones.

Patrick O'Sullivan SJ, *Prayer and Relationships*, 2008

God searching for me

In the first place, it should be known that if a person is seeking God, his Beloved is seeking him much more. This incomprehensible one takes the first initiative, he is the hunter, the Hound of Heaven who pursues us out of love. He longs to take his own inner riches and pour his whole self into our created capacities for him, into bottomless caverns of our intellect and will and memory, faculties made for him.

The question is not 'How am I to find God?' but 'How am I to let myself be found by God?' The question is not 'How am I to know God?' but 'How am I to let myself be known by God?' And, finally, the question is not 'How am I to love God?' but 'How am I to let myself be loved by God? God is looking into the distance for me, trying to find me, and longing to bring me home.'

Henri Nouwen, *The Return of the Prodigal Son*, 1994, p. 106

Passion is God's fire in us

'Long before we do anything explicitly religious at all, we have to do something about the fire that burns within us. What we do with the fire, how we channel it, is our spirituality.

Ronald Rolheiser, *Seeking Spirituality*, 1998

> The grace of God
> has always been there ahead of our preaching ...
> Hence our preaching is not really
> an indoctrination with something alien
>   from outside,
> but the awakening of something within,
> as yet not understood
> but nevertheless really present.

Karl Rahner, *Mission and Grace*, vol. 1, 1963, p. 156

---

[4] Ronald Rolheiser, *Forgotten Among the Lilies*, 2005, p. 61.

> You do not have to change for God to love you.
> Be grateful for your sins. They are carriers of grace.
> Say goodbye to golden yesterdays –
> or your heart will never learn to love the present.

Tony de Mello SJ, in Michael Harter (ed.), *Hearts on Fire*, 1993, p. 33

To have a tender moment is to pray … To pray always, as Jesus says, implies that we read the signs of the times, that we look at the conspiracy of accidents which shape our lives and read in these the finger and providence of God. The language of God is the experience that God writes into our lives.

Ronald Rolheiser, *Forgotten Among the Lilies*, 2005, p. 122

A passion for God

Why are the saints so full of passion, so ardent with desire? Because they discovered a simple truth. Desire for God, intense hunger for God, finally brings us to God. God is fire. God does not warm the tepid. God is passion. God knows nothing of half-hearted love.

Terrance W. Klein, *Vanity Faith*, 2009, p. 16

What about the passion seeping through the following prayer from the 2003 Christmas edition of *Madonna*? It comes from Daniel O'Leary's *Spirituality*.

'When you hear the Angelus bell, remember these things – I became like you on that first Christmas night, so that all of you could become like me. And so the bell will ring to shock you with the extent of my obsession with you. You are the rhythm of my breathing; the apple of my eye. You are the lines on the palms of my hands. My love for you knows no bounds. There is nothing I will not do for you. My wildest pleasure happens when you allow me to love you.'

God remembers us

[It is] helpful to jettison the picture of grace as an object and try to think of grace as an event. It's that moment when we recognize the presence of God in our lives, when finally, and all too briefly, we realize that God has always been there working on our behalf.
Terrance Klein, *Vanity Faith*, 2009, p. 24

If God ceased thinking of me, God would cease to exist.
Angelus Silesius, 17th century German mystic

Does a woman forget her baby at the breast? ... Yet even if these forget, I will never forget you.
Isaiah 49:15

God is looking into the distance for me, trying to find me, and longing to bring me home.
Henri Nouwen, *The Return of the Prodigal Son*, 1994, p. 106.
(Cardinal Basil Hume, when reflecting on the parable of the Prodigal Son in Luke chapter 15, claims that Luke 15:20-21 are the most important verses in the Bible.)

Eternal life

To live in hearts we leave behind is not to die.
Thomas Campbell, *Hallowed Ground*, quoted in
Joan Chittister, *In Search of Belief*, 1999, p. 176

Eternal life is not some great surprise that comes unannounced at the end of our existence in time; it is, rather, the full revelation of what we have been and have lived all along.
Henri Nouwen, *Life of the Beloved*, 1993, p. 107

Salvation is not some kind of religious 'goodie' that drops down from heaven to be appropriated along with other advantages in life. Nor – though Luke retains the transcendent dimension – is it simply a state or destiny awaiting individuals when they die. Salvation concerns the whole of life and begins here and now.
Brendan Byrne sj, *The Hospitality of God*, 2000, p. 5

[It was] Luke's conviction that 'salvation' is not simply something objective, 'outside' people, so to speak. It has to do with conversion at depth. People are 'saved' when they *know* reconciliation through and through in their hearts.
Brendan Byrne sj, *The Hospitality of God*, 2000, p. 28

Salvation is not only a goal for the after life. Salvation is a reality of every day that we can taste here and now.
Henri Nouwen, *Can You Drink the Cup?*, 2001, p. 91

Searching

The emotional and physical crises that interrupted my busy life at Daybreak compelled me ... to return home and to look for God where God can be found – in my own inner sanctuary. I am unable to say that I have arrived; I never will in this life, because the way to God reaches far beyond the boundary of death.
Henri Nouwen, *The Return of the Prodigal Son*, 1992, p. 17

On the day that you cease to change you cease to live.
Anthony de Mello sj

[Religions] begin to preach a spirituality of denial, rather than a spirituality of balance. They infect the world with a spirituality of fear, rather than a spirituality of joy. They want people to give things up, rather than to learn to use them rightly.
Joan Chittister, *Called to Question*, 2004, p. 220

> Let nothing disturb you,
> Let nothing cause you to fear,
> All is passing:
> God never changes.
> Patience gains all.
> Whoever has God wants for nothing;
> God alone suffices
>
> St Teresa of Avila, Prayer for Freedom

Ignatius of Loyola discovered the hard way that the issue of following Jesus is not one of giving up all that one has, but of allowing God to wean us away from our inordinate attachments (wealth, reputation, family, health, and even life itself) … That is, we pray to have our inordinate attachments removed, but we leave it up to God whether we keep the object of our attachment or not.
W. Barry SJ, *Now Choose Life*, 1990, p. 84

It took my father a long time to settle into marriage, and my mother learned the hard way, as she once told me, that the only way to hold on to those you love is to let them go. As of this writing, they've been at it for going on fifty-eight years.
Kathleen Norris, *The Cloister Walk*, 1997, p. 84

Over the years I have come to realize that the greatest trap in our life is not success, popularity, or power, but self-rejection.
Henri Nouwen, *Life of the Beloved*, 2001, p. 27

We are intimately loved long before our parents, teachers, spouses, children and friends loved or wounded us. That's the truth of our lives. That's the truth I want you to claim for yourself. That's the truth spoken by the voice that says, 'You are my Beloved.'
Henri Nouwen, *Life of the Beloved*, p. 30

To grow beyond self-rejection we must have the courage to listen to the voice calling us God's beloved sons and daughters, and the determination always to live our lives according to this truth.
Henri Nouwen, *Bread for the Journey*, 1997

For a very long time I considered low self-esteem to be some sort of virtue ... But now I realize that the real sin is to deny God's first love for me, to ignore my original goodness.
Henri Nouwen, *The Return of the Prodigal Son*, 1992

Forgiveness

If we are to love as Jesus loved, we need to be forgiving people. Forgiving people are bridge-builders, reconcilers. On this theme of forgiveness and bridge-building, let me share with you some beautiful writing by Mary McAleese, President of the Irish Republic, when she describes the remarkable reaction of one Gordon Wilson to the brutal killing of his daughter:

It is a rare person who arrives at that state of perfect spiritual serenity. I suppose they are saints of sorts, not necessarily beatified and canonised saints but the kind of people in whose presence we intuit the nearness of God because they bring their best friend everywhere with them. God does not accompany them as a bodyguard or go in front of them like a Soviet tank. He accompanies them like a soprano's pure voice accompanies a song, like a dewdrop sits on a rose.

One such was Gordon Wilson. He was a man so practised in the discipline of love that when his beautiful daughter Marie died, hard and cruelly, at the slaughter that was the Enniskillen bombing, her hand in his as she slipped away, the words of love and forgiveness sprang as naturally to his lips as a child's eyes are drawn to its mother. His words shamed us, caught us off guard. They sounded so different from what we expected and what we were used to. They brought stillness with them. They carried a sense of the transcendent into a place so ugly we could hardly bear to watch.

But he had his detractors and unbelievably his bags of hate mail. How dare you forgive, they shouted. What kind of father are you who can forgive your daughter's killers? It was if they had never heard the command to love and forgive anywhere before. It was as if they were being spoken for the first time in the history of humanity and Christ had never uttered the words, 'Father, forgive them for they know not what they do.' As one churchgoing critic said to me on the subject of Gordon Wilson, 'Sure the poor man must have been in shock', as if to offer love and forgiveness is a sign of mental weakness instead of spiritual strength.'

Mary McAleese, *Unreconciled Being: Love in Chaos*, in Desmond Tutu, *No Future Without Forgiveness*, 1999, pp. 122-123

Widely confused with forgetting or reconciliation, forgiveness is neither. It is not something we do for others; it is a gift to ourselves ... Some form of forgiveness is the end point of grieving.

Gordon Livingston, *Too Soon Old, Too Late Smart*, 2005

Heaven and hell

In Joan Chittister's book, *In Search of Belief*, she writes:

Once we turn away from childish notions of heaven, we find it where it has always been – inside ourselves. Because God is, heaven is – like God – everywhere. A disappointed disciple, the Talmud teaches, seeing studious rabbis pouring over the Torah in a plain anteroom of heaven, asks of the angel who is conducting him through paradise, 'Are those sages in heaven?' And the angel answers him, 'Oh, no, friend. The sages are not in heaven. Heaven is in the sages.'

In Search of Belief, 1999, p. 50

Gardens have a way of reminding us that death is never forever, no matter what it is that we think we have lost. 'All shall be well, and all manner of things shall be well,' Julian of Norwich wrote … It is learning to believe that in the end 'all shall be well' that may really be the central task of life … I must come to realize that all of life is part of the beauty of life. Otherwise, in the desire to be somewhere else, I may miss where I am – and what I am, as well.
Joan Chittister, *Called to Question*, 2004, pp. 189-190

No less a person than St Catherine of Siena said once: 'All the way to heaven is heaven.'

Hell is a description for people who have become comfortable with nothingness, with non-life, even a dead existence, while even being content with it. It is all they ever knew or ever expected.
Richard Rohr, *Things Hidden*, 2008, p.171

If, as Doctor Johnson said, 'the prospect of being hanged in the morning wonderfully concentrates the mind', recalling our mortality can be a healthy realism in an age when we spend so much time, energy and money denying death.
Kathleen Norris, *Dakota: A Spiritual Geography*, 2001, p. 172

In Charles Ringma's book on Henri Nouwen, *The Seeking Heart* (2009), the following line from Nouwen captured my attention: 'One of the great challenges of the spiritual life is to receive God's forgiveness. There is something in us humans that keeps us clinging to our sins and prevents us from letting God … do all the healing, restoring and renewing.'

Sin and repentance

One of the graces for which we pray in the first week of the *Spiritual Exercises* of St Ignatius is to see ourselves as loved sinners. Sadly, many retreatants seek to forget about the key word 'loved' and want to cling to their sins. Clingers are clangers, however.

Sin is my shadow side = the fact that I have not lived in harmony with whom I really am – that is, my Principle and Foundation.

In the New Testament the Greek word for 'sin' is *hamartia*. In archery it means 'missing the mark'.

What mark do we miss when we sin? Is not our mark the whole direction of our life?

'I was created to share my life and love with God and others …' (*Spiritual Exercises,* 'First Principle and Foundation').

Repentance is not a popular word these days, but I believe that any of us recognize it when it strikes us in the gut. Repentance is coming to our senses, seeing, suddenly, what we've done that we might not have done, or recognizing, as Oscar Wilde says in his great religious meditation, *De Profundis,* that the problem is not in what we do but in what we become.
Kathleen Norris, *The Cloister Walk*, 1997, p.165

How can I find God?

The book *How Can I Find God?* (2004) is a fine collection of reflections on that very question edited by James Martin SJ. Not surprisingly, it contains a splendid piece of writing by Joan Chittister OSB which is pertinent to this first Canopy here:

God is not in the whirlwind, not in the blustering and show, Scripture teaches us. God is in the breeze, in the very atmosphere around us, in the little things that shape our lives. God is in the contradictions that assail us, in the circumstances that challenge us, in the attitudes that impel us, in the motives that drive us, in the life goals that demonstrate our real aspirations, in the burdens that wear us down, in the actions that give witness to the values in our hearts.

Brennan Manning has written: 'Salvation is not reserved for the future alone. It is present when a family sits down at a family celebration in thanksgiving for the goodness they have received and the goodness they contribute to each other and enjoy fine food and good wine and great company.'

Brennan Manning, *A Glimpse of Jesus*, 2004,

The loquacious man

I have been a Catholic since 1956, when I was baptised wearing a white dress. My forebears, family, friends, schools, and employers were Catholic. Catholicism was my language, my coat, my house. I learned to pray in two American Catholic tongues, Latin and English, and to relish the smoky poetry of the Mass, an ancient ritual prayer. I chanted the rosary with my brothers and sister, I prayed to Saint Francis when I found the huddled corpses of sparrows, I prayed to Saint Blaise when my throat burned.

When I was twelve, my grandmother shrivelled and died and I prayed desperately for her soul during her funeral Mass, a sad waltz that taught me the enormous power of ritual, the skeleton that sustains us when we are weak.

Then I stopped praying. It seemed pointless, a speech delivered to an empty room, a plea without ears.

Many years passed. I grew up. Slowly, I began to hear and see and taste prayers: a fox against snow, my wife's hand, my mother's corduroy voice. One morning on an island I went to get my mail and two purple finches flew out of the mailbox and I knew that they were prayers.

One day, years later, a cold doctor said to me, 'You will never have children', and that night I opened my mouth and prayed to the woods and skies and birds, to the shambling God I could not find but sensed everywhere, and since that day I have prayed silently and aloud, with my hands and feet, with my heart.

It seems to me now that all things are prayers. Curiosity and memory and silence and water are prayers. People are prayers. I have a daughter now, two years old, an exuberant prayer. We talk about God, whom she calls Gott. When she is asleep, my wife and I cover her with one blanket and two prayers.

As a boy I learned the names of the boxes that prayers are mailed in: the Our Father, the Hail Mary, the Mass of the Dead. I learned to hate the boxes because they seemed empty, mere strings of dusty words. I did not see that they are a means to an end, and that the end is a piercing conversation with Gott, the man who is nowhere and everywhere, who is not a man, who was a man, who never stops talking."

Brian Doyle, 'The Loquacious Man' from *Two Voices*, 1996*

---

*Reproduced by kind permisssion of the author.

With Jesus on the road

Jesus is the great love letter of God. He cannot deceive, cannot be incomplete. The love of God has been encoded into his very flesh.
Terrance Klein, *Vanity Faith,* **p. 90**

Jesus, the Lamb, turns towards these first two disciples
  and asks:
'What are you looking for?' (John 1:38)
These are the first words of Jesus in this gospel.
Perhaps they are the first words of Jesus to each one of us.
Jesus does not want to impose on us an idea,
  a doctrine or an ideology.
He wants people to follow him and his path of love freely.
He calls us to look into our own hearts
and to become aware of our fundamental desires.
What do we really want for our lives?
What are we looking for?'
Jean Vanier, *Drawn into the Mystery of Jesus through the Gospel of John*, 2004, pp. 37-42

Some questions

There are in fact three questions that Jesus puts to us in the adventure of discipleship of him. We encounter him, and grow in our encounter of him, to the extent that we hear these questions and allow three questions to disturb us. They are, in fact, not questions that can be answered easily. However, it's in our very struggle to answer the questions that our experience of Jesus begins to deepen.

The first ... is the question that he asks the very first disciples ... 'What do you want? What are you looking for?' This is what Jesus constantly asks us, 'What do you desire?'...

As we allow ourselves both to hear and to struggle with this question, Jesus puts another one to us, however. 'Who do you say I am?' (Mark 8:29) ...

There is a third question that Jesus puts to his disciples ... 'Do you love me?' There is an understanding that only comes through the risk of loving. Only as we are drawn to love Jesus, to surrender in commitment and trust, do we really come to know him.

David Ranson, 'Faith Formation in Our Encounter with Jesus', a a paper delivered to an Ignatian Formation planning meeting at Peter Canisius House CIS, Pymble, 19 July 2016

Specifically, we will explore our identity, calling and unique place in the larger scheme of God's creation. These are basic questions of life and spirituality:

'Where do I fit?'

'Why am I here?'

'Most fundamentally, who am I?' ...

I believe that God patiently and gently invites me to the continual work of singing and playing my song in the world ... In essence, this re-connection with your name, your song and your original purpose is the core of spirituality.

Jerry Webber, 'Listening for Your Name: Hearing Your First Purpose' – a splendid article from the United Methodist Church, Houston, Texas – see www.chapelwood.org

The mind and heart of Christ

What is the mind and heart of Christ? It is the acceptance of the fact that everyone is special and therefore all are equal. Nobody sits above the rest and nobody has a right to feel that he or she should sit above the rest. This is true for nations as well as for individuals. If individuals accepted this there would be much less jealousy, competition and violence among us. If nations accepted it, our world would not be poised on the brink of economic and nuclear destruction. Show me a good loser and I will show you a loser! Jesus was a good loser. In his underachieving we all achieved salvation. In his mind and heart lie the seeds that can bind us into one heart beyond jealousy, competition and violence.
Ron Rolheiser, 'In Exile' column, *Western Catholic Reporter*, 1 March 1985

To be a fool for Christ's sake means to risk being honest in a world where dishonesty seems in favour, being courageous where caution is a way of life. Those who choose to follow Jesus will suffer some dying, but death is not what they choose.
W. Barry sj, *Now Choose Life*, 1990, p. 95

Freedom and trust

The immediate result of attempting to live Jesus' spirituality today is freedom. We learn gradually to let go, to free ourselves from our attachments, to throw away our crutches, to ignore our need for success, and to liberate ourselves from worries about reputation. Fears, worries, obsessions, and compulsive behaviour begin to fade into the background as we learn to laugh at our egos. For some, the greatest relief of all is the experience of freedom from guilt. Our wrong-doing will never be held against us. We are forgiven. We are free.

Discovering the truth about ourselves begins the process of personal liberation. Discovering the truth about today's world, an open and honest recognition of what is happening in the human world and in the universe as a whole, can be a liberating experience. The truth will set you free….

The basis of radical freedom is trust. We become free as we gradually learn to appreciate God's love for us, which leads us to surrender ourselves and to put all our trust in God.
Albert Nolan, *Jesus Today*, 2006, pp. 181-182

Although I have not been able to check it out, two different scripture scholars have told me that Jesus is asked 183 questions directly or indirectly among the four gospels. Do you know how many of these he directly answers? Three! Jesus' idea of church is not about giving people answers but, in fact, leading them into liminal and dark space, where they will long and yearn for God, for wisdom and for their own souls.
Richard Rohr, 'We need transformation, not fake transcendence', *NCR*, 15 February 2002

It took half a life time to get to the point where fear no longer held my soul in thrall to the God of the system, but captive instead to the God of the woman taken in adultery.
Joan Chittister, *Called To Question*, p. 39

The Baptism of Jesus is a tale of intimacy.
Kathleen Norris, *The Cloister Walk*, 1997, p. 108

'You are my beloved Son, on you my favour rests' (Mark 1:11). This was a blessing, and it was that blessing that sustained Jesus through all the praise and blame, admiration and condemnation that followed.
Henri Nouwen, *Life of the Beloved*, pp. 59-60

Jesus and ourselves

And, dear friends, if there is anything I want you to hear, it is that what is said of Jesus is said of you. You have to hear that you are the beloved daughter or son of God. And to hear it not only in your head but in your gut, to hear it so that your whole life can be turned around.
Henri Nouwen, sermon, 'Being the Beloved', 1992

We do not simply become the beloved at our birth and cease being the beloved at our death. Our belovedness is eternal. God says to us: 'I love you with an everlasting love.'
Henri Nouwen, *Here and Now*, 1994

Becoming the beloved means letting the truth of our belovedness become enfleshed in everything we think, say, or do. It is a long and painful process of ... incarnation.
Henri Nouwen, *Life of the Beloved*, 1993

Jesus has to be and to become ever more the centre of my life. It is not enough that Jesus is my teacher, my guide, my source of inspiration ... Jesus must become the heart of my heart, the fire of my life, the lover of my soul, the bridegroom of my spirit.
Henri Nouwen, *Jesus and Mary*, 1992

God-with-us

In his book, *Already Within*, Daniel O'Leary recalls an experience of trying falteringly to console some young parents whose baby had just died in Leeds Hospital, before the father took his wife in his arms and said: 'You know I love you.' He writes:

My understanding of Incarnation now is that such moments are the only ones in which God can touch and hold us, redeem and

> save us, console and empower us. The way the Word-become-Flesh heals and restores happens in no other situation than in the human interplay of senses, emotions and physical relationships … such are the only moments in which our incarnate God can be intimate with us. Is this not the reason behind Karl Rahner's famous definition of sacraments as 'celebrations of what is already there in human experience'?
>
> Daniel O'Leary, *Already Within*, 2007

The wonderful feast of Christ the King tells us what sort of king Jesus was. He was not a King over land or territory, but he was a King of Hearts. The only power he had was the power of love. This feast of Christ the King, King of Hearts, asks all of us the question: What rules our heart? What motivates us, moves us, what drives us along in life and how? What and whom do we make time for?

During his time as head of Catholic Adult Formation, Sydney priest Monsignor Tony Doherty wrote some very thoughtful articles. One line that has stayed with me was his conviction that 'Christians must be owners not blamers'. It is so true. If we look at the gospels closely, we can see that Jesus was prepared to judge people constructively, but not condemn them.

'Go and sin no more', Jesus says to the woman caught in adultery in that beautiful scene in chapter 8 of John's Gospel. While He does not condone her action in any way, Jesus places her wellbeing before the letter of the law. He sets her free to take ownership for her actions, but there is no hint of blame or dismissal. Jesus always places people before the law. Jesus offers healing not blame. Christians are on about owning, not blaming.

The two standards – two flags

The flag bearer is the pivotal person in the formation of an army. St Ignatius asks us to reflect and discern:

> Do we place ourselves behind the standard/flag of Jesus Christ?
> Or, do we place ourselves behind the standard/flag of Satan?
> Riches – honours – pride?

St Ignatius makes the point that we need to be constantly aware that it is easy to slip from one standard/flag to the other in our life … if we are not discerning, constantly on the lookout.

The Trinity

The Feast of the Trinity celebrates the fact that God is always much more than our pictures and words for him. In contrast to what the fundamentalists and extremists might think, God cannot be watered down or controlled by any religious formulations. Ultimately, God the Trinity is much more than our descriptions, because God is mystery.

To use Gerard W. Hughes' term, God is 'a beckoning word', constantly inviting us to travel beyond our narrowness to encounter him in awe and wonder. The all-embracing imagery of my Celtic cross reminds me of the fact that the Trinity is all around us:

> The sacred Three
> My fortress be,
> Encircling me.
> Come and be round
> My hearth and my home.
> Fend Thou my kin
> And every sleeping thing within
> From scathe, from sin.

> Thy care our peace
> Through mid of night
> To light's release.

Celtic 'Blessing of the Three'

Jesus in our world

'Can we see Christ in the world?' The answer is, 'No, we cannot see Christ in the world, but only through the Christ in us can we see Christ in the world.' The answer reveals that the Christ within us opens our eyes to the Christ among us.
Henri Nouwen, *The Road to Peace,* 1998

The loaves and the fishes – The Lord is so good. Brothers and sisters, when you hold on to what you have, it always gets less. When you give away what little you have, it always multiplies, whether it is food or knowledge or affection or love.
Henri Nouwen, *The Road to Peace,* 1998

Dear Lord, help me to keep my eyes on you. You are the incarnation of divine love, you are the expression of God's infinite compassion, you are the visible manifestation of God's holiness. You are beauty, goodness, gentleness, forgiveness and mercy. In you all can be found … Let me give you all – all I have, think, do and feel. It is yours, O Lord. Please accept it and make it fully your own. Amen.
Henri Nouwen, *A Cry for Mercy,* 1981

The truth that sets people free is so capacious that we have to walk around it many times to take in all its facets and dimensions … Perhaps Jesus preferred to speak in parables to keep his truth from immediately set in stone, memorized or owned. He expected his disciples to have to chew on them a while to unlock their flavor.
Michael Heher, *The Lost Art of Walking on Water,* 2004, pp. 132-133

Because fundamentalists are such fearful people, hell bent on control rather than grace, they only have room for an either/or vocabulary. Theirs is talk about absolutes, black and white, with no room for grey. Why not speak this way? After all, they see themselves as the sole possessors of the truth!

Well, I happen to think that the truth requires a lifelong search and no one individual, group, or party has sole possession of it, even for a moment in time. That is called idolatry. The wonderful American writer Kathleen Norris has a good take on this when she says, 'We have become afraid of the imagination, thereby settling for false certitudes and unable to embrace ambiguity and mystery.'

> My lifetime of studying Jesus would lead me to summarize all of his teaching inside of two prime ideas: *forgiveness and inclusion* ... Forgiveness and inclusion are Jesus' 'great themes'. They are the practical name of love, and without forgiveness and inclusivity love is largely a sentimental valentine.'
>
> Richard Rohr, *Things Hidden*, p. 151

The need for both

While Jesus says in the gospel of Martha and Mary that Mary showed 'the better part' (Luke 10:42), we need *both* the contemplative and active elements in our life if we are to function properly. All of us need a contemplative balcony in life if we are to maintain some perspective on the busy-ness of its dance.

For life is a matter of both/and rather than either/or. Life is a series of combinations, of doubles: light and dark; weak and strong; ebb and flow; bread and wine; Good Friday and Easter Sunday; victory and loss; rich and poor; success and failure; rights and responsibilities; life and death; male and female; divine and human; yin and yang; the saint and the dragon; the contemplative and the active.

Jesus the lover

Jesus had always loved those who were his in the world, but now he loved them to the end.

John 13:1

*The stars shine most brightly
when the night is darkest.*

Author unknown

In the Third Week of the *Spiritual Exercises*, 'what the retreatant is called to is *not* to choose the Cross or suffering in isolation but, in the light of all that has gone before, *to choose Jesus*. It is the option of the Second Week [Canopy Two] made explicit … The sorrow, compassion and shame for which we pray (*Exercises* 193) are not ends in themselves but rather to help the retreatant "not to be deaf to his call" (*Exercises* 91)'
Philip Sheldrake, 'Theology of the Cross and the Third Week',
The Way Supplement, 1987

Do not look forward to what might happen tomorrow; the same everlasting Father who cares for you today will take care of you tomorrow and every day. Either he will shield you from suffering or he will give you unfailing strength to bear it. Be at peace, then, and put aside all anxious thoughts and imaginings.
St Francis de Sales

Too much faith in God

I saw a kind of faith once that defied all the psychology I'd ever been taught, all the theological definitions I'd ever learned. It seeped into my own faith-life like mist, illuminated the dark places, and clung to my soul like ether.

She was writhing on the floor in her bedroom by the time I got there. Her elbows were tight against her ribs, her fists were clenched, she was rolling back and forth, from side to side, and moaning. She was a gentle woman, a kind of Dresden doll. She'd been a first grade teacher all her life. She had reared generation after generation just by the lilt of her smile. Years later they were still coming back to adore her.

But she was also manic-depressive. She had been in and out of hospitals all her life, on one medication after another for years. When drugs became available the periods between the laughter and the deep, deep gloom became longer. But never permanent.

Over the years, as she got older, the chemical balance became harder and harder to maintain. Then she would become depressed to the point of heartbreak. The doctors would admit her to the hospital, withdraw her from her current medicine, and, only when she was completely purged of a previous drug, start again to find the right dosage for the new prescription. It took a long time to do. They were frightening and painful periods for her. The pain, the gloom, the despair, the depression, the writhing, all became part of the routine.

But for all the regularity of it, I had never seen her this bad before. I got down on my knees beside her and took her by the shoulders. 'Come on, Theresie,' I said. 'Time to go to the doctor again.' The wail came from the centre of her. 'No!' she insisted. 'No! Don't make me do that. I can't do that. I hate that.' I began to rock her a little. 'Theresie,' I crooned, 'the doctor is worried about you. He wants you in the hospital.' She stiffened. 'I know he's worried,' she sobbed. 'He won't believe me. He thinks I want to commit suicide! I've tried to explain to him but he won't listen.'

She shuddered a deep breath. 'Joan, tell him. Tell him! I would never do that. I have too much faith in God to do that!' I couldn't see her for the tears in my own eyes. She was a holy woman and I knew she was telling the truth. She really did have too much faith in God to do that. She knew she was not being punished, not being abandoned, not being tested, not being scourged. She knew she was sick and she knew that God was with her in the midst of the darkness of it.

The God who turns red lights green at our command is not the God Theresie worshipped. The God who gives points for good behaviour is not the God she knew. Her God was the loving Creator in whose energy and life 'we live and move and have our being' (Acts 17:28). Her God did not manipulate life, but rather gave it and then enabled her to live it out, learning as she went, loving as she did. Her God was the creator of the seasons – the One because of whom winter always turned into spring.
Joan Chittister, *Scarred by Struggle, Transformed by Hope*, 2003

Suffering is what we are called to transform into new life. Suffering leads us to be another part of ourselves ...Suffering pares us to the core ... exposes us to ourselves.
Joan Chittister, *Called to Question*, 2004, pp 208, 209

Hope, according to [Vaclav] Havel, is different from optimism. It is a state of the soul rather than a response to the evidence. It is not the expectation that things will turn out successfully but the conviction that something is worth working for, however it turns out. Its deepest roots are in the transcendental, beyond the horizon.
Seamus Heaney, *Finders Keepers*, quoted by Bill Barry in *Human Development*, Spring, 2003, p. 3

Struggle

All addictions make us slaves, but each time we confess openly our dependencies and express our trust that God can truly set us free, the source of our suffering becomes the source of our hope.
Henri Nouwen, *Life of the Beloved*, 1993, p. 80

… our wounds are often an essential part of the fabric of our lives.
Henri Nouwen, *Life of the Beloved*, 1993, p. 81

The crucified Jesus reminds us that in weakness and vulnerability God's love can shine forth mightily. The Risen Jesus reminds us that our hope rests in his power over death and his continued identification with those who bear his name.
Decree 1, par. 9, Documents of General Congregation 34, 1995

The real presence of God

Occasionally when St Augustine handed the Eucharist to a communicant, instead of saying, 'the Body of Christ' he would say, 'Receive what you are.' Augustine had perceived, for whatever reasons, that the words of consecration, 'This is my body, this is my blood', are intended more to change the people present than to change the bread and wine. For him it was more important that the people became the real presence of God, that they became food and drink for the world, than that the bread and wine did. That is, in fact, the real task of the Eucharist: to change people, to create out of us the real presence.
Ronald Rolheiser, *Forgotten Among the Lilies*, 1990, p. 183

Chris …. during some dark days in Boarding, you reminded me that Good Friday is always followed by Easter Sunday. I am now taking this same message to the next school assembly.
An excerpt from an Easter note written to me by a former staff member who was in his first year as principal of a Catholic school

When the night has been too lonely and the road has been
    too long,
And you think that love is only for the lucky and the strong.
Just remember in the winter, far beneath the bitter snow,
Lies the seed that, with the sun's love, in the spring becomes
    the rose.
Bette Midler's famous song, *The Rose*

Those who have a 'why' to live can bear almost any 'how'.
Friedrich Nietzsche, quoted by Viktor Frankl in
Man's Search for Meaning

Lord, help me to remember
that nothing is going to happen to me today
that you and I together cannot handle.
'Old preacher's prayer', author unknown (see Matthew 6:25-34)

In the midst of Jesus' anguished prayer asking his Father to take his cup of sorrow away, there was one moment of consolation. Only the evangelist Luke mentions it. He says: 'Then an angel appeared to him, coming from heaven to give him strength' (Luke 22:43). In the midst of sorrows is consolation … The cup of sorrow … is also the cup of joy.

Henri Nouwen, *Can You Drink the Cup?* 1996

Good Friday

Today [Good Friday], the primary human problem, the core issue that defeats human history, is both revealed and resolved. It is indeed a 'good' Friday. The central issue at work is the human inclination to kill others, in any multitude of ways, (physically, sexually, emotionally, mentally, spiritually …) instead of dying ourselves – to our own illusions, pretences, narcissism, addictive and self-defeating behaviours. *Jesus dies to save us from ourselves!*

Jesus dies 'for' us not in the sense of 'in place of' but *in solidarity with*. 'In place of' is merely a heavenly transaction of sorts; 'in solidarity' is about transformation. The soul needed one it could 'gaze upon' long enough to know that it was *we who were doing the 'piercing' (John 19:37) and we who were being pierced in doing it*. Jesus' body is a standing icon of what humanity is doing and what God suffers 'with', 'in', and 'through' us. It is an icon of utter divine solidarity with our pain, our 'issues' and our problems.

In the cross of Christ Jesus, our crosses are absorbed and transformed.

Whenever you see an image of the Crucified Jesus, it reveals what humanity is doing to itself and to one another. It is you and every person and Jesus all at the same time. *Don't lessen its meaning by making it merely into a mechanical transaction whereby Jesus pays some 'price' to God or the devil.* The only price paid is to the human soul– so it can see what it has done, who it is, and what it still can be.

Don't lessen its meaning by making it into a mechanical transaction whereby Jesus pays some 'price' to God or the devil.

As Franciscan scholar John Duns Scotus taught, Jesus did not need to die. *There was no debt to be paid.*

'Learning from the cross', *Everyday Catholic*, March 2001

The cross makes everything clear

Nothing changed in heaven on Good Friday, but everything potentially changed on earth. Some learned how to see and to trust the relationship between God and humanity. God has always and forever loved what God created, 'it was always good, it was very good' (Genesis 1:31). It was we who could not love and see God's inexhaustible goodness. *Jesus died to reveal the nature of the heart of God.*

The cross makes everything clear. The mystery of the rejection, suffering, passion, death and rising of Jesus is the fuel of human history. *We are wounded, and we are transformed.* Whenever you see an image of the Crucified Jesus, it reveals what humanity is doing to itself and to one another. It is you and every person and Jesus all at the same time. *'The cross proves everything.'*

Jesus calls us, asks to follow him on the journey of transformation. Our job is, quite simply, to be Jesus. And yet we admit we don't know how to be Christ Jesus. Christ Jesus has to do it in us, through us. All we can do, is get out of the way and let the mystery of the cross absorb our suffering and struggle and transform us.

Adapted from Richard Rohr's *Wondrous Encounters*, 2010

The gaunt man

Years ago, on a wet Easter morning, I found a fallen sparrow chick on the concrete floor of the garage. It was a male, about a week old. He was twisted, small, deceased. Some time during the night he had fallen or been shoved by his siblings from a dishevelled nest in the eaves.

My brothers and I buried him in a crayon box and prayed over the gaudy coffin. My youngest brother sobbed convulsively. The broken chick did not rise from the dead, as we hoped but did not expect. Ever after, says my brother, he looked upon Jesus with a jaundiced eye, and questioned the potency of a story that could not stir life in something so small as a shrivelled sparrow.

I have wondered at that story, too. It was the epic of my youth: a magic birth on a crystalline night, a precocious boy in a temple, water and blood, a dusty murder on a dark afternoon – and the final thrilling detail, an empty tomb where the dead man had been, its huge stone door flung aside like a pebble.

It was the first story I knew well, the first tale in which I could hear the clash and ring of history and sin. Its hero – gaunt, wrapped in a long white cloak, dusty feet in dusty sandals – fascinated me, and I studied his legend, pored over the disparate accounts of his brief life, strained to hear divine music in his odd stories. I tried, fitfully, to emulate his patience, generosity and courage. But mostly, as I grew older and more suspicious of magic, I forgot him, although he hovered at the edge of consciousness and memory, sad-faced and haunted, a gaunt bearded man who died young and was probably God.

Not until I turned thirty-three did I finally taste the sour evil of his death on my tongue, and sense the real horror of his murder. For a Catholic boy, that age is one of power and resonance, of inevitable measurement against that lost life, of stock taken; and over the course of that year I found myself thinking about the carpenter more than I expected to and more than I wanted to. I found myself staring at his story in the oddest moments: on the train, in the woods, in the cobbled alleys of my ancient city. I couldn't get over the stark fact of his death, which stuck out like the ribs of a malnourished child.

A quiet carpenter is arrested, spiked to a cross, and left to die. Dust and a strange darkness swirl at his feet. His mother weeps; his best friend watches in helpless silence. Twilight crawls over the nearby hills. He cries aloud with thirst, despair, terror; and he dies. Three days later he is seen, on the road. He walks, he talks, he allows a skeptic to plunge a thumb into his wounds. He disappears again, but this time the fierce story of his life and death remains in the air, outlined by the blood and tears of those who knew him. The story spreads and takes on a life of its own, filling the earth. Two thousand years later the carpenter's story, unaccountably powerful, still haunts the world.

And it haunts me.

Stories are powerful, weighty things. They have lives of their own. Woven of memory and desire, they begin with an ungainly parade of facts in the same way that a sparrow chick is made up of downy uncertainty, splayed feet and hunger. With time they acquire grace beyond their ingredients, and meaning beyond the hole they occupy in the freighted air.

I have my own story, in which compassion and mercy and humor salve a little of the evil I find in my city, in my work, in the twisted people and ashen faces that pass me in the street. In my middle years I look for God in the carved faces of my elders and the translucent faces of the young, in joy and sadness, in gain and loss, in the eyes of fish, the boles of oaks, the runes left by the feet of birds. I have fled from the crutch of faith, the evil of religion too tightly held, the intolerance of the confident, because it is subtlety that seems holy to me, not assurance; because those men and women most sure of themselves and their gods often seem furthest removed from godlike peace and mercy.

But always the carpenter's story whispers to me. It is as haunting as love, as persistent as doubt. For years I have dodged in and out of it like a child on the bright thin edge of a forest, immersed in it when it suited me, ignoring it when it did not. Now I face it with awe and fear and pity. In the piping voices of children, in the hollow voices of beggars, in the savage barking of guns in alleys, I hear the ragged voice of the man on the cross, raging at his betrayal, offering his broken soul to the harsh God he called his father.

I don't know if that man was the lord of time and space and mercy. No one knows; no one will ever know, not in this life. You bet your life on him or you don't; you walk into his story, wondering at its astonishing power, leery of its simplicity and enormous demand, or you walk away from it because it is impossible to believe or live by. Like a mountain, a cathedral, a sparrow, the story of the gaunt man is a vaulting thing, impossible to ignore.

I am afraid of his story because I suspect that it is true.

Brian Doyle, 'The Gaunt Man' from *Two Voices*, 1996*

---

*Reproduced by kind permisssion of the author.

Canopy four

God the giver and the gift

> *The resurrection of Jesus is not about 'resuscitation' ... not about revivification of an old life ... [it] is about coming to grips with the transformed and transforming presence of Christ then, now, and always.*
>
> Joan Chittister, *In Search of Belief,* 1999, pp. 133, 134

> *Read again Jesus' questioning of Peter in John chapter 21. 'The question is not: How many people take you seriously? How much are you going to accomplish? Can you show some results? But: Are you in love with Jesus?'*
>
> Henri Nouwen, *In the Name of Jesus*, 1989

The German philosopher and atheist, Friedrich Nietzsche, said once about Christianity: 'If you want me to believe in your redeemer, then you've got to look a lot more redeemed.' Some who profess to be Christians believe, mistakenly and sadly, that there is no place for fun in religion. So steeped in their attachment to sin are these unfortunates that they overlook religion as our connection to God and others.

Fun connects us. Sin disconnects. It's the wrong focus and it shows in such people's demeanour. Instead of coming to Communion to partake joyfully in the hospitality of God the Host, their faces reveal the sort of misery and gloom that envelops constant watchers of television news. They have forgotten that Christians are meant to be people of the resurrection, incurable optimists who keep on believing, trusting, hoping, and working for the possibility of change.

Episcopal priest Morton Kelsey said it beautifully: 'In spite of all the evidence to the contrary, in spite of all the evil in us and around us, God is love.'

Christopher Gleeson sj, *The Front Page*, ATF, 2011, pp. 139-140

> How lovely is the sun after rain,
> and how lovely is laughter after sorrow

Tunisian proverb

Joy and laughter

The joy of the resurrection means, as Sebastian Moore states (in *Jesus the Liberator of Desire*, 1989, p. 57), that 'life is no longer lived under the shadow of death, it is in the light with death behind us. The virus of eternity has entered our bloodstream for ever.'

W. Barry sj, *Now Choose Life*, 1990, p. 98

A praising of God is what laughter is, because it lets a
    human being be human.
Laughter is a praise of God, because it lets a human being
    be a loving person.
Laughter is praise of God because it is a gentle echo of God's
    laughter, of the laughter that pronounces judgment on
    all history.

Laughter is praise of God because it foretells the eternal praise of
God at the end of time, when those who must weep here
   on earth shall laugh.
The laughter of unbelief, of despair, and of scorn, and the laughter
of believing happiness are here uncannily juxtaposed, so that
before the fulfilment of the promise, one hardly
   knows whether belief or unbelief is laughing.
God gave us laughter – we should admit this and laugh.
Karl Rahner in his meditation on 'Mardi Gras', quoted in Kathleen Norris, *Amazing Grace*, 1998, pp. 357, 358

The laughter of human beings must correspond to something in God. He shares our sorrows; he must also share our laughter, so I prayed to recognize the wink of God and to hear his laughter in my own and other people's seriousness and solemnity.
Gerard W. Hughes, *Walk to Jerusalem*, 1998, p. 135

Of the heart

Golf, of course, is a deeply spiritual game. British Jesuit and spiritual author, Gerard Hughes, was once hacking his way around a course in the company of his nephew, a very accomplished golfer. After watching his uncle playing like the perfect professional's partner, his nephew gave him two very important pieces of golfing and spiritual advice: 'Uncle Gerard, if you want to improve, you have to keep your head down and your hands aligned to your heart.' What excellent advice for golfers and all of us trying to grow in the spirit! As St Augustine said so beautifully: 'And he departed from our sight that we might return to our heart, and there find him.' What we do with our hearts can change the universe.
Christopher Gleeson SJ, *The Front Page*, ATF, 2011, pp. 125-126

Easter joy

Easter is a powerful reminder that we cannot take God's limitless love for granted. We simply cannot afford to omit the words 'thank you' from our vocabulary. A few years back, ABC journalist Caroline Jones, wrote these beautiful words about the significance of Easter:

This weekend, millions of Christians will go to their churches to enter into the 2000-year-old story of Jesus Christ, man of love, nailed to the cross, dead, buried, and amazingly risen to life. Embarrassing as the claim may be in a scientific age, when this cross is placed as a template of meaning on the many small 'deaths', the crises and disappointments of human life, it offers a way out of despair to hope. Of every bewilderment, the Christian can ask, not the defeating 'why', but instead the hopeful: 'Where in this pain is the seed of life?'

Song of the Virgin Mary

My soul proclaims the greatness of the Lord,
My spirit rejoices in God my Saviour,
for you, Lord, have looked with favour on your lowly servant.
From this day on all generations will call me blessed.
The Almighty has done great things for me;
Holy is your name.
You have mercy on those who fear you
in every generation.
You have shown strength with your arm
and scattered the proud in their conceit,
casting down the mighty from their thrones
and lifting up the lowly.
You have filled the hungry with good things
and sent the rich away empty.

You have come to the aid of Israel, your servant,
to remember the promise, the promise of mercy –
the promise which was made to our forebears,
to Abraham and his children forever.
Luke 1: 46-55

Patient trust

Above all, trust in the slow work of God.
We are all, quite naturally,
impatient in everything to reach the end
without delay.
We should like to skip
the intermediate stages.
We are impatient of being
on the way to something unknown,
something new,
and yet it is the law of all progress
that it is made by passing through
some stages of instability –
and that it may take a very long time.

And so I think it is with you.
Your ideas mature gradually –
let them grow,
let them shape themselves,
without undue haste.
Don't try to force them on,
as though you could be today
what time (that is to say, grace and
circumstances acting on your own good will)
will make you tomorrow.

> Only God could say what this new spirit
> gradually forming within you will be.
> Give our Lord the benefit of believing
> that his hand is leading you
> and accept the anxiety of
> feeling yourself in suspense and incomplete

Pierre Teilhard de Chardin, *Letters 1914-1919*, in Michael Harter SJ (ed.), *Hearts on Fire: Praying with the Jesuits*, 1993

Be on the watch

Watch your feelings: they become your thoughts.
Watch your thoughts: they become your words.
Watch your words: they become your actions.
Watch your actions: they become your habits.
Watch your habits: they become your character.
Watch your character: it becomes your destiny.
Author unknown

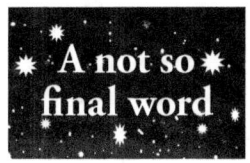

A not so final word

I am always nervous about writing 'a final word', so I have changed it to 'a not so final word.' Stopping still on the journey is to go backwards. Indeed, formation of whatever nature is always a work in progress. Pope Francis said it well in one of his homilies in March 2013: 'Our life is a journey, and when we stop moving, things go wrong.'

For six weeks in 2016 – from late April to early June – I was given the wonderful opportunity to participate in an Ignatian Immersion program in Manresa, Spain. Manresa, of course, is in the heart of Basque country – the place where St Ignatius of Loyola began to cobble together his rich experiences of God, that later were printed as the *Spiritual Exercises* and have since been life-changers for thousands of people across the globe.

Some thirty-four immersion participants from fifteen countries became pilgrims in heart, mind and body as we probed deeper into the spirituality and story of Ignatius and his first companions. The teaching and course work, our silent retreat, the community fellowship, the pilgrimages to Montserrat, Loyola, Xavier and Barcelona, not only contributed to us learning more about Ignatius the Pilgrim but more importantly helped us to share something of his ardent love for Jesus.

On 30 April I had the privilege of celebrating Mass for the group at the former hospital and chapel of St Lucia – now known as the Chapel of the Rapture – where St Ignatius spent a good deal of his time during his eleven months at Manresa in 1522. In my homily, referring to Ignatius' fondness for the designation 'Pilgrim', I spoke about the metaphor of the pilgrim as a very helpful one for us journey-men and women in life.

Somewhere in his prodigious writings, the former Chief Rabbi of the Commonwealth, Jonathan Sacks, distinguishes between the pilgrim and the tourist. Pilgrims are those people who want to engage with the world and not be mere spectators, people whose goal is less to reach a particular destination than to be transformed in the journey itself. A tourist goes somewhere to see something new, while a pilgrim goes somewhere to *become* someone new. Indeed, tourism protects tourists from becoming someone new by insulating them from the unfamiliar or the uncomfortable.

In an excellent article on 'Humility: A Pilgrim's Virtue', Lisa Fullam points out that the pilgrim is a risk-taker.

> The mark of a pilgrim, then, is vulnerability but also receptivity, openness to the gifts offered along the way. A pilgrim's journey is a vote of confidence that God will look out for the wandering stranger as God cared for Israel in the desert … Humility begins with the acknowledgement that we are vulnerable.

Many moons ago, in my year of ordination, I read a splendid homily by Michael Buckley SJ to my American Jesuit ordinand companions in which the homilist challenged them: 'Are you weak enough to be a priest?' It reminded me of Paul's second letter to the Corinthians where he claims stridently: 'For it is when I am weak, that I am strong' [with God's grace] (2 Corinthians 12:10).

If we are to move forward in caring for people, we need to be at ease with a vulnerability that makes us dependent on God. A Sunday newspaper caption today says it well: 'In painful moments, trust in God. In every moment, be grateful.' What a wonderful way to move forward!

Let us end with the words often attributed to that intrepid explorer, Sir Francis Drake:

> Disturb us, Lord, when
> We are too well pleased with ourselves,

When our dreams have come true
Because we have dreamed too little,
When we arrived safely because we sailed too
    close to the shore …
Disturb us, Lord, to dare more boldly,
To venture on wider seas
Where storms will show your mastery;
Where, losing sight of land,
We shall find the stars.

References

Please find below details of the books and articles referred to throughout this book. We have endeavoured to find accurate references for all quotations, and would appreciate any help in making these as correct as possible.

W. Barry sj, *Now Choose Life: Conversion as the Way to Life*, Paulist Press, Mahwah, 1990.
Louis de Bernières, *Captain Corelli's Mandolin*, Vintage, London, 1998.
Brendan Byrne sj, *The Hospitality of God: A Reading of Luke's Gospel*, St Pauls Publications, Sydney, 2000.
Dom Helder Camara, *A Thousand Reasons for Living*, DLT, London, 1984.
Thomas Campbell, *Hallowed Ground*, quoted in Joan Chittister, *In Search of Belief*, Ligouri, Ligouri, 1999.
Joan Chittister, *Called to Question: A Spiritual Memoir*, Sheed & Ward, New York, 2004.
Joan Chittister, *In Search of Belief*, Ligouri Publications, Ligouri, 1999.
Joan Chittister, *Living Well: Scriptural Reflections for Every Day*, Orbis Books, 2000.
Joan Chittister, *Scarred by Struggle, Transformed by Hope*, Eerdmans, Grand Rapids, 2003.
Joan Chittister, *Songs of Joy: New Meditations on the Psalms for Every Day of the Year*, Crossroad, New York, 1997.
Pierre Teilhard de Chardin, *The Divine Milieu*, HarperSanFrancisco, 1960.
Pierre Teilhard de Chardin, from *Letters 1914-1919*, translated by Michael Harter sj, *Hearts on Fire: Praying with Jesuits*, Loyola Press, Chicago.
Bryce Courtenay, *A Recipe for Dreaming*, Heinemann, Melbourne, 1994
Stephanie Dowrick, *Forgiveness and Other Acts of Love: Finding True Value in Your Life*, Penguin, Australia, 1997.
Jim Doyle & Brian Doyle, *Two Voices: A Father and Son Discuss Family and Faith*, Ligouri Pub;lications, 1996.

Dag Hammarskjöld, *Markings* (23/6/57), Knopf, New York, 1964.
Cardinal Basil Hume, *In My Own Words*, Hodder & Stoughton, 1999
Tony de Mello SJ, from *Hearts on Fire: Praying with Jesuits*, Michael Harter SJ (ed.), Loyola Press, Chicago, 1993.
Viktor Frankl, Man's Search for Meaning, Beacon Press, Boston, 1959.
Lisa Fullam, 'Humility: A Pilgrim's Virtue', *New Theology Review*, 19, May 2006.
Kahlil Gibran, *The Prophet*, Knopf, New York, 1923.
Christopher Gleeson SJ, *The Front Page*, ATF, Adelaide, 2011.
Michael Harter SJ (ed.), *Hearts on Fire: Praying with Jesuits*, Loyola Press, Chicago, 1993.
Seamus Heaney, *Finders Keepers: Selected Prose, 1971-2001*, quoted by Bill Barry in *Human Development*, Spring, 2003.
Michael Heher, *The Lost Art of Walking on Water: Reimagining the Priesthood*, Paulist Press, New Jersey, 2004.
Gerard W. Hughes, *Walk to Jerusalem: In Search of Peace*, Darton Longman & Todd, London, 1998.
Cardinal Basil Hume, *In My Own Words*, Hodder & Stoughton, 1999.
Terrance W. Klein, *Vanity Faith: Searching for Spirituality among the Stars*, Liturgical Press, Collegeville, 2009.
Michael Leunig, *A Common Prayer*, Collins Dove, Melbourne, 1991.
Gordon Livingston, *Too Soon Old, Too Late Smart: Thirty True Things You Need to Know Now*, Hodder, Sydney, 2005.
Mary McAleese, *Unreconciled Being: Love in Chaos*, in Desmond Tutu, *No Future Without Forgiveness*, Penguin/Random House, London/New York, 1999.
Michael McGirr, *The Good Life*, Aurora/David Lovell Publishing, Melbourne, 2000.
Brennan Manning, *A Glimpse of Jesus: The Stranger to Self-hatred*, HarperSan Francisco, 2004.
James Martin SJ, *How Can I Find God?* Ligouri, Ligouri, 2004.
Sebastian Moore, *Jesus the Liberator of Desire*, Crossroad, New York, 1989.
Anne Morrow, Gift from the Sea, Pantheon, New York, 1983.

Albert Nolan, *Jesus Today: A Spirituality of Radical Freedom*, Orbis Books, Maryknoll, 2006

Kathleen Norris, *Amazing Grace: A Vocabulary of Faith*, Riverhead Books (Penguin), New York, 1998.

Kathleen Norris, *The Cloister Walk*, Penguin/Random House, London/New York, 1997.

Henri Nouwen, sermon, 'Being the Beloved', 1992.

Henri Nouwen, *Bread for the Journey: A Daybook of Wisdom and Faith*, HarperCollins, San Francisco, 1997.

Henri Nouwen, *Can You Drink the Cup?*, Ave Maria Press, Indiana, 1996.

Henri Nouwen, *A Cry for Mercy: Prayers from the Genesee*, Doubleday, New York, 1981.

Henri Nouwen, *Here and Now: Living in the Spirit*, Crossroad, New York, 1994.

Henri Nouwen, *In the Name of Jesus: Reflections on Christian Leadership*, Crossroad, New York, 1989.

Henri Nouwen, *Jesus and Mary: Finding Our Sacred Centre*, Franciscan Media, Cincinnati, 1992.

Henri Nouwen, *Life of the Beloved: Spiritual Living in a Secular World*, Crossroad, New York, 1993.

Henri Nouwen, *The Return of the Prodigal Son: A Story of Homecoming*, Darton Longman & Todd, London, 1994.

Henri Nouwen, *The Road to Peace: Writings on Peace and Justice*, Orbis Books, Maryknoll, 1998.

John O'Donohue, *Anam Cara: Spiritual Wisdom from the Celtic World*, Transworld, London, 1997.

Daniel O'Leary, *Already Within: Divining the Hidden Spring*, Columba Press, Dublin, 2007.

Daniel O'Leary, 'Spirituality'. See www.djoleary.com.

Patrick O'Sullivan sj, *Prayer and Relationships: Staying Connected – An Ignatian Perspective*, David Lovell Publishing, Melbourne, 2008.

Karl Rahner in his meditation on 'Mardi Gras', quoted in Kathleen Norris, *Amazing Grace: A Vocabulary of Faith*, Riverhead Books (Penguin), New York, 1998.

Karl Rahner, *Mission and Grace*, vol. 1, Sheed & Ward, New York, 1963.

Charles Ringma, *The Seeking Heart: A Journey with Henri Nouwen*, Paraclete Press, Brewster, 2009.
Richard Rohr, *Things Hidden: Scripture as Spirituality*, Franciscan Media, Cincinnati, 2008.
Richard Rohr, *Wondrous Encounters: Scripture for Lent*, Franciscan Media, Cincinnati, 2010.
Ronald Rolheiser, *Forgotten Among the Lilies: Learning to Love Beyond Our Fears*, Doubleday, New York, 1990.
Ronald Rolheiser, 'In Exile' column, *Western Catholic Reporter*, 1 March 1985.
Ronald Rolheiser 'Learning from the cross', *Everyday Catholic*, March 2001 www.americancatholic.org/Newsletters/EDC/ag0301.asp
Ronald Rolheiser, *Seeking Spirituality: Guidelines for a Christian Spirituality for the Twentieth Century*, Hodder & Stoughton, London, 1998.
Virginia J. Ruehlmann, *The Poems and Prayers of Helen Steiner Rice*, Baker Publishing, Ada, 2004.
Joyce Rupp, *Praying Our Goodbyes*, Ave Maria Press, Notre Dame, 1988.
M. Scott Peck, *Further along the Road Less Travelled: The Unending Journey Towards Spiritual Growth*, Simon & Schuster, New York, 1993.
Philip Sheldrake, 'Theology of the Cross and the Third Week', *The Way Supplement*, 58, Oxford, 1987.
Desmond Tutu, *No Future Without Forgiveness*, Doubleday, New York, 1999.
Jean Vanier, *Drawn into the Mystery of Jesus through the Gospel of John*, Novalis, Ottawa, 2004

Christopher Gleeson SJ has spent most of his working life as a teacher and administrator in Jesuit schools, nearly twenty-one of which as Head of both Xavier College in Melbourne and St Ignatius' College, Riverview, in Sydney. His peers elected him to serve as Chair of the Association of Heads of Independent Schools of Australia from 1999 to 2001. Since leaving Riverview at the end of 2002, he was Director of Jesuit Publications (now Jesuit Communications) in Melbourne, and inaugural Director of both the Faber Centre of Ignatian Spirituality and the Archdiocesan Santa Teresa Spirituality Centre in Brisbane. In January 2011, he was appointed to be the Provincial's Delegate for Education and Mission Formation, and in January 2016 took on the new role of Provincial Delegate for Ignatian Formation. Over the years he has written four books for parents and teachers – *Striking a Balance: Teaching Values and Freedom* (Aurora Books 1993), *A Canopy of Stars: Some Reflections for the Journey* (David Lovell Publishing 2003), now revised and updated within these covers, *Releasing the Angel: Saluting all who strive to teach* (Australasian Theological Forum, 2007), and *The Front Page: Everyday Ignatian Spirituality* (Australasian Theological Forum, 2011). Chris Gleeson is a member of the Australian Jesuit Province and is based in Our Lady of the Way Parish, Lavender Bay, Sydney.

www.ingramcontent.com/pod-product-compliance
Lightning Source LLC
Chambersburg PA
CBHW071230080526
44587CB00013BA/1555